The Gratitude Rese Boosting Practice

Rewire Negative Think..g, ~~Build Resilience~~ & Bring More Joy into Everyday Life

By Amelia Walsh

The Gratitude Reset: A 30-Day Mood Boosting Practice
© 2025 Amelia Walsh

This book is for informational and inspirational purposes only. The author is not a medical professional, and the practices shared here are not intended to replace medical advice, diagnosis, or treatment. Always seek the guidance of a qualified health provider with any questions you may have regarding your health or wellbeing.

Dedication

For those who are searching for light in heavy seasons,
for those who long to notice joy in the small and
ordinary,
and for those ready to begin again—

this book is for you.

And to everyone who has ever reminded me,
through kindness and presence,
that gratitude is always within reach—thank you.

About the author

Amelia Walsh is a British writer with a passion for helping others reconnect with themselves through simple, everyday mindset practices. Drawing on a background in psychology and lived experience with anxiety and burnout, Amelia writes with honesty, warmth, and a deep belief that small changes can lead to powerful transformation.

She lives in the English countryside where she finds peace in slow mornings, long walks, and the quiet joys of ordinary life. Her work invites readers to embrace self-kindness, reduce mental clutter, and find steady calm—even when life feels overwhelming.

The Gratitude Reset is her heartfelt guide to building emotional resilience through the gentle habit of noticing what's good.

Part of the *Everyday Reset* series—practical, uplifting guides designed to help you create small daily habits that lead to lasting positive change.

Foreword

When we hear the word *reset*, many of us think of technology—pressing a button to clear errors and start again. But what if we could do that for our hearts and minds? What if, instead of being swept up in stress, comparison, and constant striving, we could pause, breathe, and shift into a state of calm, connection, and joy?

That is the promise of gratitude.

For centuries, philosophers, poets, and spiritual teachers have praised gratitude as a key to happiness. In recent years, science has confirmed what wisdom traditions already knew: gratitude changes the brain, improves relationships, lowers stress, and strengthens resilience.

And yet—knowing it is one thing, practising it is another. Life is busy. Negativity is loud. It's easy to forget gratitude in the rush of daily living.

That's why this book matters. *The Gratitude Reset* is not about abstract theory—it's a guide for living gratitude in real, tangible ways. It's practical, simple, and deeply human. Through stories, reflections, and a 30-day step-by-step plan, you'll discover how gratitude can move from an idea in your head to a rhythm in your life.

As you read, you'll see that gratitude doesn't require perfect circumstances. It can be found in the middle of difficulty, in the smallest details, and even in the most ordinary days. This is gratitude not as a quick fix, but as a reset—a way to return, again and again, to what matters most.

May this book be a companion on your journey. May it remind you that joy is closer than you think. And may it help you find gratitude not just once, but every day.

Contents

Part One – Foundations of Gratitude

Introduction: You're Not Broken — You're Just Human

If you're holding this book, chances are you're feeling stretched thin. Maybe you wake up already tired, your brain buzzing with a to-do list that feels longer than the day ahead. Maybe you keep scrolling through other people's highlight reels and wonder why, despite everything you're doing, you still feel like something's missing. On the outside, you may look like you've got it all together. Inside, though, it's a different story.

Let me say this clearly: you are not broken. You are human.

And being human in today's always-on world is exhausting. We're living in a culture that trains us to chase more, achieve more, compare more—and still feel like it's never enough. It's no wonder so many of us feel disconnected, anxious, or stuck in a fog of stress.

But here's the quiet truth: normal doesn't mean inevitable. Just because this is common, doesn't mean it has to stay this way.

What This Book Isn't

This isn't about plastering on a fake smile or pretending everything is fine when it's not. It's not about toxic positivity—the kind that tells you to "look on the bright side" while ignoring your real struggles. And it's not about turning gratitude into another chore on your already overloaded list.

Instead, this is about something much simpler—and far more powerful.

Gratitude.

Not the fluffy kind. Not the "post a quote on Instagram" kind. But the kind that roots you, quietly and honestly, in the small good that's already here. The kind that shows up in the laugh you didn't expect, in the comfort of a warm drink, in the fact that despite everything—you're still standing.

Why Gratitude?

I didn't choose to write about gratitude because life was perfect. Quite the opposite. Gratitude became my anchor in seasons when everything felt like too much. Anxiety. Burnout. Loss. Days when my inner critic was loud and life felt heavy.

What surprised me was that gratitude didn't erase the hard parts—it sat alongside them. It whispered: "Yes, this is tough. And also... not everything is broken." That small shift changed how I related to stress, how I connected with others, and how I began to feel at home in myself again.

That's why I want to share it with you. Because gratitude isn't a personality trait. It's a practice. And it's one anyone can build, no matter where you're starting from.

The Everyday Reset Approach

This book is part of the *Everyday Reset* series—a collection of gentle, practical guides to help you create small daily habits that actually last. The idea is simple:

real change doesn't come from massive overhauls. It comes from tiny, honest shifts you can stick with.

In this reset, you'll learn how to:

- Interrupt spirals of negative thinking
- Rewire your brain for more calm and clarity
- Find joy in ordinary, overlooked moments
- Build resilience for life's harder seasons
- Create a daily gratitude habit that takes minutes, not hours

You don't need to be naturally optimistic. You don't need a perfect morning routine. You don't even need to feel grateful right now. You just need a willingness to notice one small good thing at a time.

A Fresh Lens, Not a Fresh Start

This isn't about starting over. You don't need to reinvent yourself. What you need is to change the lens through which you see your days. Gratitude is that lens.

When you shift how you notice, everything else shifts too. A day that felt ordinary begins to feel meaningful. A season that felt overwhelming becomes survivable. A life that felt heavy starts to feel lighter—without anything "big" changing at all.

An Invitation

So here's my invitation to you:

- Put down the pressure to "get it right."

- Let go of the myth that gratitude only counts if it's written in a perfect journal.

- Begin exactly where you are, even if where you are feels messy.

This is not about perfection. It's about presence.
Not about ignoring pain, but about noticing what's still good, right here, right now.

You're not broken. You're human. And with a few gentle resets, you can feel more grounded, more connected, and more alive.

Let's begin.

If you're holding this book, chances are you're feeling stretched, tired, or like something's missing—despite the fact that from the outside, you may seem like you've got it all together.

You're busy. Your brain won't switch off. You wake up already thinking about the to-do list. And somewhere in between work meetings, laundry, social obligations, and the endless scroll of other people's highlight reels—you've lost touch with a sense of *you*. That quiet feeling that everything is OK. That you're *OK*.

And here's the thing: you're not alone. And you're certainly not broken.

In fact, what you're feeling is incredibly normal in today's always-on world. But normal doesn't mean it has to stay this way.

This book isn't about pretending everything's fine when it's not. It's not about toxic positivity or forcing a smile when all you want is five minutes of silence and a cup of tea. This is about something far more powerful—and far more realistic.

Gratitude.
Not the fluffy kind. Not the Instagram quote kind. But the *real* kind. The kind that sneaks up on you when your dog does something daft. When your child laughs from their belly. When you finally take a deep breath and realise you're still here, still standing.

This book will show you how to see those moments—not just once in a while, but every day. And in doing so, you'll build something better than just a "gratitude habit." You'll begin to rebuild *connection*—with yourself, your life, and the parts of your day you've been rushing past.

You don't need a fresh start or a complete overhaul. You just need small, honest shifts that remind you of the good that's already here. Right now.

Let's begin.

Chapter 1 – Why Gratitude Works (Even When Life's a Mess)

You don't need a perfect morning routine, a quiet mind, or a shiny new journal to begin practising gratitude. You don't even need to feel happy first. Gratitude doesn't wait until life is tidy—it grows in the middle of the mess.

In fact, the mess is often where gratitude matters most.

Gratitude Isn't Just About Feeling Grateful

When you're burnt out, grieving, or stressed to the point of snapping, someone telling you to "just be grateful" can feel dismissive. Gratitude has been misused—treated as a quick-fix soundbite, or worse, as a way of silencing pain.

But authentic gratitude doesn't deny your struggles. It sits alongside them.

You can be grateful and grieving.
You can feel anxious and still appreciate the calm of a hot shower.
You can be angry and still notice the way sunlight falls across your kitchen floor.

Gratitude isn't about forcing a smile. It's about creating an anchor—a thread of steadiness you can hold when everything else feels shaky.

What Gratitude Actually Does in Your Brain

It's not just poetic—it's neurological. Gratitude literally rewires your brain.

When you pause to notice what's good, even for a few moments, your brain activates the prefrontal cortex (responsible for calm, reasoning, and perspective) and dials down the activity of the amygdala (the fear centre). In simple terms: gratitude helps you step out of panic mode and into steadier ground.

Even small acts—like writing down three things you're grateful for—boost the release of dopamine and serotonin, two mood-regulating chemicals. Over time, your brain starts to carve new pathways that make it easier to notice positives automatically.

Research backs this up:

- A study from UC Davis found that people who kept a daily gratitude journal for ten weeks reported better sleep, fewer physical complaints, and more optimism compared to those who didn't.

- Harvard researchers discovered that gratitude activates brain regions linked with reward and bonding, making it easier to feel both joy and connection.

- Neuroscientist Alex Korb describes gratitude as a "natural antidepressant" because of the way it increases resilience against stress and lifts mood over time.

But the evidence doesn't stop there. In a 2020 meta-analysis published in *Frontiers in Psychology*, researchers found that gratitude interventions significantly reduced symptoms of anxiety and depression across more than 4,000 participants. Even brief daily reflection exercises had measurable benefits within two weeks.

A team at the University of Zurich went further: brain scans showed that consistent gratitude practice led to longer-term changes in the ventromedial prefrontal cortex—the area associated with emotional regulation and moral reasoning. In other words, gratitude doesn't just make you feel better temporarily; it reshapes how your brain processes future experiences, helping you interpret challenges through a calmer, kinder lens.

There's also an impact on the body. Gratitude stimulates the parasympathetic nervous system—the "rest and digest" response—helping to lower heart rate and blood pressure. Over time, this physiological shift contributes to better immune function and reduced inflammation. So when you practise gratitude, you're not only changing your thoughts—you're quite literally altering the chemistry of your wellbeing.

Gratitude doesn't erase life's difficulties, but it strengthens the internal systems that help you recover from them.

But What If Life Feels Too Hard?

One of the most common questions people ask me is:

"How am I supposed to be grateful when I'm overwhelmed, grieving, or exhausted?"

My answer: this is exactly when gratitude is made for you.

Gratitude doesn't erase pain. It simply reminds you of what's still here. Even on the hardest days, it can sound like:

"I got through today, even if it wasn't pretty."
"I have clean water and a place to rest."
"I cried, but I also laughed for a moment."

Tiny acknowledgements like these matter. They don't cancel the hard parts—but they stop the hard parts from being the only parts.

Psychologists sometimes call this "cognitive broadening." When stress narrows your focus to threat, gratitude widens your attention again. You begin to notice small resources—people, comforts, routines— that were invisible under strain. That widening is the first step back to balance.

Gratitude vs Toxic Positivity

It's important to draw a line here.

Toxic positivity tells you to "look on the bright side" at all costs. It dismisses suffering and pressures you to act cheerful when you're not.

Gratitude, by contrast, is honest. It says:

"Yes, this is difficult. And also, here's one thing that's still good."

That dual awareness—pain and possibility—creates space for healing. Gratitude doesn't silence your story; it expands it.

Gratitude Doesn't Require Big Moments

We often think gratitude is reserved for weddings, promotions, sunsets, or birthdays. But true gratitude lives in the small, ordinary details.

The warmth of tea in your favourite mug
The smell of fresh laundry
A dog wagging its tail when you come home
The relief of sitting down after a long day
A kind word from a stranger

These tiny moments are powerful because they give your nervous system a chance to reset. They're not insignificant—they're medicine for the mind.

The more you notice them, the more your brain learns to scan for what's working instead of only spotting what's missing. Over weeks and months, this becomes self-reinforcing: positivity bias replacing negativity bias. You begin to *expect* good, and that expectation itself subtly improves mood, motivation, and social connection.

Debunking the Myths About Gratitude

Let's clear away some common myths:

Myth 1: "I have to feel happy first."
Truth: Gratitude isn't a reward for happiness—it's a tool to help create it.

Myth 2: "It only counts if I journal."
Truth: Writing helps, but gratitude can also be spoken aloud, texted to a friend, whispered before bed, or felt in your body.

Myth 3: "If I'm grateful, I'll stop trying to improve my life."

Truth: Gratitude fuels growth. It keeps you grounded while you reach for more. When you start from enoughness, effort feels lighter and more sustainable.

Myth 4: "I'll fail at it like everything else."
Truth: Gratitude is not a performance. It's a practice. Imperfect is normal. Inconsistent is human. Every time you return to it, you're succeeding.

Why This Book Exists

This book isn't here to make your life perfect. It's here to help you see it differently—to show you that even in the chaos, there is still good, and that noticing it can change how you feel day to day.

You don't need hours of free time or endless energy. You just need a willingness to pause. Each chapter in this book will guide you to bring gratitude into real life: into your busy mornings, your workdays, your relationships, and especially into the hard times.

Because gratitude isn't about changing who you are. It's about reconnecting with what's already here.

Reflection & Action Prompt

Today's Challenge:
Before you go to bed tonight, name three things you're grateful for. Keep them small and specific. Then, ask yourself why each one mattered.

Example:
"I'm grateful for my cup of tea—because it gave me five minutes to breathe."
"I'm grateful for a text from my friend—because it reminded me I'm not alone."

"I'm grateful for my warm bed—because it's my place of rest."

Notice how this feels in your body. That's your nervous system shifting, even just a little.

Chapter 2 – From Auto-Pilot to Awareness

Why You Don't Notice the Good (Yet)

Most of us live on auto-pilot far more than we realise.

You wake up, check your phone, rush through breakfast, half-listen to the news, juggle emails, jump into meetings or errands, cook, clean, care for others—and suddenly it's 9 p.m. You're exhausted, but when you look back on the day, it feels like a blur. What did you actually enjoy? What moment made you smile? Often, the answer is… you can't remember.

It's not your fault. The modern world is wired for distraction. Notifications pull you one way, responsibilities another. There's always a message to respond to, a task to finish, a headline demanding attention. Life becomes a constant hum of "next thing, next thing, next thing." In the rush, your attention narrows to problems, pressures, and deadlines—while the quieter good moments slip past unnoticed.

And here's the real problem:
When you don't notice the good, your brain assumes it isn't there.

Over time, this creates an invisible imbalance. Your nervous system becomes tuned to threat and urgency rather than calm and appreciation. You might still have hundreds of tiny moments of beauty—sunlight through a window, laughter, a moment of kindness—but they pass through you unregistered. Gratitude can't exist where awareness hasn't yet landed.

The Science of Auto-Pilot

Your brain runs on two main systems that constantly trade places throughout the day:

1. **Habit Mode (Auto-Pilot)** – Controlled mainly by the basal ganglia. This is the part that lets you drive to work without thinking about every turn, or make tea without concentrating. It's wonderfully efficient, saving mental energy for complex decisions. The downside? It also means you can drift through entire days half-asleep to your own life.

2. **Awareness Mode (Presence)** – Centred in the prefrontal cortex, this system helps you pay attention, reflect, make decisions, and connect meaningfully with the world around you. It uses more energy, which is why your brain defaults to auto-pilot whenever possible. It's a clever survival tactic—but not a recipe for happiness.

In evolutionary terms, this automatic functioning kept our ancestors safe. You needed your attention free to spot danger or opportunity, not to admire the clouds. But in a world of constant stimulation, that same system now keeps us trapped in reactive mode. We're running on habits that help us *function*, but not necessarily *feel alive*.

Here's where gratitude comes in. Gratitude acts like a mental "switch." When you pause to notice something good—no matter how small—you reactivate the prefrontal cortex. That moment of appreciation literally changes your brain's activity pattern, pulling you out of the habit loop and back into awareness. Over time, repeated gratitude strengthens the neural pathways associated with attention, emotional regulation, and calm.

Neuroscientists describe this process as *neuroplasticity*—the brain's ability to rewire itself through repeated experience. Each time you catch yourself noticing the good, even briefly, you are teaching your mind a new direction of focus. You're saying, in effect, *this matters*. And your brain listens. With enough practice, awareness becomes not an effort, but a default way of being.

It's a beautiful paradox: the more you notice, the easier noticing becomes.

The Hidden Cost of Living on Auto-Pilot

It's tempting to think auto-pilot is harmless—after all, you're still functioning, getting things done, meeting deadlines. But living disconnected has a cost that often sneaks up on you.

- You stop noticing beauty in ordinary moments.

- You feel reactive instead of reflective.

- You forget to celebrate small wins.

- You start to believe life is just a cycle of stress and survival.

- Joy becomes rare, fleeting, or something you think you'll "get to later."

This mental drift creates a kind of low-grade fog. You might not even realise how dulled you've become until something jolts you—illness, loss, burnout—and suddenly you long for the simple peace you didn't know you were missing.

Gratitude is like opening a window—it clears the air and lets the light back in. A single conscious breath of appreciation can interrupt the grey routine of a day and remind you that, beneath the noise, your life still holds moments of gentleness and meaning.

Psychologists sometimes refer to this state of constant low awareness as *attentional fatigue*. When your focus is hijacked by multitasking and stress, the brain's reward circuits flatten. Nothing feels satisfying for long. Gratitude, by sharpening focus on what's already enough, acts as a natural antidote to that dullness.

Five Signs You're Stuck on Auto-Pilot

1. You finish eating but barely tasted your food.

2. You scroll through your phone but can't recall what you saw.

3. You drive somewhere but don't remember the journey.

4. You reply "yes" automatically, without considering what you want.

5. You look back on the day and can't remember one thing that made you feel alive.

If even one of these feels familiar, you're not failing— you're simply human in a distracted age. Our minds are designed to wander; awareness is a skill we must keep re-learning. That's why gratitude matters so much. It's not about being endlessly positive; it's about returning, over and over, to the living moment.

Awareness Isn't Complicated (But It Is Powerful)

Becoming more present doesn't require hours of meditation or a silent retreat in the mountains. You don't need special equipment or endless free time. You just need willingness to pause and notice what's already here.

Think of awareness as the doorway; gratitude is what steps through it.

Here are three easy awareness practices you can try today:

- **Look for sensory detail.** What can you smell, hear, touch, or taste right now that feels comforting? The softness of your jumper, the smell of coffee, the warmth of your tea. Engaging your senses pulls you out of rumination and back into your body, where calm naturally resides.

- **Notice transitions.** The quiet between meetings. The pause before you enter a room. The moment your head hits the pillow. These liminal spaces— those "in-between" moments—are perfect anchors for gratitude because they're often overlooked.

- **Catch micro-moments.** The sound of birdsong. A smile from a stranger. The sigh of relief when you finally sit down. These tiny flashes are where joy often hides. By catching them, you train your brain to find small positives without effort.

None of these are "big" moments. And yet they matter—because they gently bring your brain back to the present, reminding you that life is still happening *now*, not later. When you build this muscle of noticing, gratitude begins to flow naturally, not as an obligation but as a quiet response to being awake to your own life.

Case Story: Sophie's Red Light Reset

Sophie used to describe her mornings as "one long rush".

She'd wake up already tense, mentally scrolling through her to-do list before her feet even touched the floor. The drive to work was the worst part. Every red light felt like a personal insult. She'd tap the steering wheel, sigh heavily, mutter under her breath, and arrive at her desk already frazzled.

When Sophie first tried practising gratitude, she didn't think it would help. "I'm too busy for all that journaling stuff," she said. But instead of forcing a formal routine, she decided to start small—just a pause at every red light.

At first, it felt awkward. Her brain kept racing ahead: *emails, deadlines, errands.* But over the next few days, something shifted. She began using those brief moments of stillness to look around: the sky's soft colour before 9 a.m., the music playing quietly on the radio, the warmth of her coffee in the cup holder.

By the end of the first week, she wasn't dreading the lights anymore. They'd become tiny invitations to breathe.

This is the hidden power of awareness—it doesn't demand more time; it simply changes how you use the time you already have.

What Sophie was really doing was rewiring her stress response. Each time she paused to notice the good, she interrupted her habitual tension pattern. Her body moved from the stress-driven *sympathetic* state (fight or flight) into the *parasympathetic* one—the system that restores calm and balance. Over time, these micro-pauses became her nervous system's cue for safety.

When I asked Sophie how it felt after a month, she said something simple but profound:

"The red lights didn't change. I did."

That single sentence captures the heart of gratitude practice. The world rarely slows down for us—but awareness allows *us* to slow down inside it.

Even small, consistent acts like Sophie's "red light reset" retrain the brain's attentional bias. Instead of scanning the environment for obstacles and irritations, your brain starts to scan for what's steady, comforting, or beautiful. And because what we focus on expands, life begins to feel subtly kinder.

Micro-Moments Multiply

Sophie's story might sound simple, but the ripple effect was enormous.
That one mindful shift changed the texture of her mornings. She arrived at work less reactive, more focused, and surprisingly, more patient with colleagues. She wasn't just calmer—she was *clearer*.

This is what researchers call **cognitive flexibility**: the ability to shift perspective easily. Gratitude strengthens this skill by giving your brain practice in seeing more than one reality at a time—the stress *and* the small peace, the difficulty *and* the quiet grace. Over time, it becomes easier to recover from setbacks and adapt to challenges.

So while Sophie's "red light reset" took less than a minute, the emotional benefits lasted all day. The brief awareness pause created momentum. Gratitude doesn't have to be grand to be powerful; it just has to be consistent.

When you begin noticing small joys in predictable places—like the morning commute, your first sip of tea, or the hush before sleep—you're not escaping responsibility. You're reconnecting with your *capacity to feel alive within it.*

Awareness Is the Doorway to Gratitude

Every practice in this book begins here: noticing. You can't feel grateful for what you haven't first seen. That's why this chapter focuses on awareness—it's the gateway through which gratitude flows.

The next time you catch yourself running on auto-pilot, try a mini "reset" moment of your own. It doesn't need to be perfect or profound. You might take a deep breath while waiting in a queue, feel the texture of your jumper, or simply notice the light changing through the window.

What matters isn't the moment—it's your attention.

Every time you shift from rushing to noticing, you strengthen the same mental muscles Sophie used at those red lights. Over weeks and months, those small resets accumulate. One day, you'll realise you're not racing through life quite so blindly. You're present for it—and that, in itself, is gratitude in action.

The Gratitude Shift

Once you start noticing more, something subtle but extraordinary begins to happen:
your inner dialogue changes.

Gratitude isn't just about spotting the good—it's about shifting the lens through which you see the world.

Psychologists sometimes call this *cognitive reframing*: learning to interpret experiences through a broader, more balanced perspective rather than defaulting to negativity or threat.

When you're caught in habitual stress or self-criticism, your brain filters reality through what's known as the *negativity bias*—a built-in survival mechanism that prioritises danger and mistakes over calm or pleasure. It kept our ancestors safe, but it can quietly rob modern life of joy. Gratitude challenges that bias. It doesn't pretend problems don't exist; it simply insists they are not the whole story.

Every time you choose to acknowledge something positive, you are training your mind to hold two truths at once:

"This is hard, **and** there's still something good here."

That tiny **and** is the hinge upon which gratitude turns.

How Reframing Works

Think of reframing as giving your thoughts breathing space. It's not about denying emotions or forcing silver linings; it's about expanding your perception so that pain doesn't occupy the entire view.

For example:

- "I have so much to do today" becomes "I have a full day because people trust me to get things done."

- "It's raining again" becomes "The plants, the garden, the earth needed this."

- "I'm exhausted" becomes "I gave my energy to things that mattered."

Each shift is small—sometimes only a sentence apart—but the emotional impact can be profound. It's not the event that drains you most; it's the meaning you attach to it.

The human mind is constantly making meaning. We interpret, label, and judge almost every moment of experience, usually without noticing. Gratitude helps you become aware of those interpretations and choose gentler ones. You're not editing out reality—you're *including* more of it.

Over time, gratitude reshapes what psychologists call your **explanatory style**—the habitual way you explain events to yourself. People with a more grateful explanatory style tend to view setbacks as temporary and specific ("this was a difficult day") rather than permanent and global ("my whole life is falling apart"). This shift alone has been linked with greater resilience, lower anxiety, and a higher sense of meaning.

In a 2019 study from the University of Nottingham, participants who practised daily gratitude reframing for just two weeks showed increased optimism and reduced rumination compared to a control group. Their stress levels didn't vanish, but their interpretation of stress changed—they felt more capable of coping. That's the gratitude shift in action.

The Language of Lack vs the Language of Enough

If you listen closely to your inner voice, you might notice that much of our self-talk is written in the *language of lack*.

"I should be further ahead."
"I never get a break."
"I always mess things up."

These words—*should, never, always*—are small but powerful. They harden the edges of your experience, turning temporary moments into fixed truths.

Gratitude invites you to rewrite those scripts in the *language of enoughness*:
"I'm learning at my own pace."
"I'm grateful for the quiet moments I do get."
"I made a mistake, but it's not the end of the story."

This isn't forced positivity—it's psychological realism. You're training your brain to register the full picture, not just the parts coloured by fear or frustration. As clinical psychologist Rick Hanson often says, "The brain is like Velcro for the bad and Teflon for the good." Gratitude, quite simply, helps the good stick.

From Awareness to Appreciation

Awareness opens the door; gratitude walks through it. The more you notice, the more opportunities you create to shift perspective.
That might mean pausing mid-task to appreciate that you're capable, even when tired, or catching yourself before you spiral into self-criticism and choosing a gentler thought instead.

Gratitude doesn't erase reality—it reframes it in a way that keeps your heart open.
It turns *pressure* into *presence*, *obligation* into *opportunity*, and *comparison* into *contentment*.

The real miracle isn't that life suddenly improves—it's that your relationship with life does.

As the writer Melody Beattie once put it:

"Gratitude turns what we have into enough."

That single sentence sums up the gratitude shift: a quiet transformation from chasing what's missing to noticing what's already here.

The 5-Minute Habit

By now, you've seen how easily awareness can slip away and how gratitude can bring it back. But insight alone doesn't create change. What transforms awareness into lasting calm is repetition — small, deliberate moments of noticing, done consistently enough that they become part of who you are.

That's where the **five-minute habit** comes in.

It sounds almost too simple: spend just five minutes a day paying attention to what's good. But those five minutes are a kind of mental weightlifting. Each repetition strengthens the neural pathways that make appreciation easier the next time.

The goal isn't to add another task to your to-do list; it's to build a rhythm that fits naturally into the life you already live.

Why Five Minutes Works

Psychologically, the shorter the habit, the less resistance your brain creates. When a task feels easy, you're more likely to start — and starting is 90% of success.

Behavioural scientist BJ Fogg calls this the *tiny habits effect*: small, achievable actions that build momentum.

Gratitude works the same way. Writing down ten things can feel overwhelming when you're tired, but noticing one or two small moments? That's manageable.

Five minutes is also long enough for your nervous system to register safety. As you slow your breathing, reflect, or write, your heart rate settles and the body shifts from "doing mode" into "being mode". Even this brief pause can lower cortisol, boost serotonin, and reset emotional balance for the rest of the day.

Think of it as pressing "save" on the day's best moments before they vanish.

How to Begin

There's no single right way to practise the five-minute habit — what matters most is consistency. Here are a few gentle options:

1. **The Morning Grounding.**
   Before you reach for your phone, name three things you're grateful for. Keep them small and sensory: the softness of your pillow, the quiet before the world wakes, the smell of coffee brewing. This sets a calm baseline before the rush begins.

2. **The Midday Pause.**
   Stop at some natural transition — lunch, a walk, or a red light like Sophie's. Ask yourself, *What's one thing that's going well right now?* Even if it's tiny ("I finished a tricky email" or "the sky looks beautiful"), you're teaching your brain to re-anchor mid-flow.

3. **The Evening Reset.**
   Before bed, reflect on what went right today. You could jot it in a notebook, voice note it, or simply replay moments mentally. Gratitude at night helps your mind settle, creating a stronger sense of closure and more peaceful sleep.

You can rotate these options or choose one anchor time that suits you best. Consistency builds faster when you link the habit to something that already happens daily — what behavioural experts call *habit stacking*.

For example:
"After I brush my teeth, I'll name one thing I'm grateful for."
"After I switch off my computer, I'll pause and thank myself for something I did well."

The cue triggers the habit automatically, until it becomes second nature.

Making It Stick

To make any new habit last, focus less on *perfection* and more on *pattern*.
You don't need to do it at the same time every day, or write beautifully worded lists. Even pausing for thirty seconds counts. What matters is returning, again and again.

You can make your practice more tangible by using one of these light structures:

- A **small notebook** by your bed or kettle — so gratitude becomes part of winding up or winding down.

- A **notes app** or digital list titled *Moments That Matter*.

- A **visual cue** — like a candle, a shell, or a post-it on the mirror — that reminds you to pause.

The key is to remove friction. The easier it is to begin, the more your brain will repeat it.

And if you miss a day? Simply start again. Habits built on self-kindness last far longer than those built on guilt.

Identity Over Outcome

The true goal isn't to "complete" a gratitude list — it's to become the kind of person who notices good things. Each five-minute practice is a vote for that identity.

James Clear, author of *Atomic Habits*, puts it perfectly: "Every action you take is a vote for the type of person you wish to become." When you choose to pause, reflect, or give thanks, you're reinforcing the belief: *I am someone who appreciates life as it happens.*

That shift in identity — quiet, almost invisible — is what creates lasting change.

You may not see results instantly, but over weeks, those five-minute practices accumulate. You'll start to find yourself noticing more without effort: the taste of food, the feeling of sunlight, the relief of laughter. Your brain begins to expect goodness instead of overlooking it.

This is how gratitude becomes not an exercise, but a way of seeing.

A Simple Template to Try

If you'd like a gentle structure, you can follow this five-line format. Keep it quick and imperfect:

1. **Today I'm grateful for...** (list one or two things)

2. **Because...** (why it mattered — this deepens meaning)

3. **One small thing I learned or noticed...**

4. **One small act of kindness I gave or received...**

5. **How I want to carry this feeling forward...**

That's it. Five lines, five minutes, one small daily reset.

Gratitude isn't about changing your life overnight — it's about changing the *quality* of how you live it, five minutes at a time.

Reflection & Action Prompt

Your challenge:
For the next three days, commit to a single five-minute gratitude habit.
Don't overthink it — pick a time, keep it simple, and notice how it feels.

By the end of those three days, you'll likely find that awareness feels easier, calmer, and somehow richer. That's not coincidence — that's your brain beginning to remember how to notice the good.

Chapter 3 – The Gratitude Shift: Changing the Lens

From Scarcity to Enough

Gratitude changes everything — but not in the way you might expect.
It doesn't erase stress, or turn problems into rainbows overnight. What it does is far quieter and far more powerful: it changes the way your mind interprets reality.

When you begin practising gratitude, you start to notice something fascinating. The world around you hasn't changed — the same routines, people, responsibilities — but *your experience* of it softens. What once felt grey begins to hold small sparks of warmth. You catch yourself smiling at moments that used to rush past unnoticed.

This is **the gratitude shift** — the slow rewiring from *scarcity thinking* to *enoughness*.

For most of us, scarcity thinking is our default setting. It's the constant whisper of *not enough* that hums in the background of everyday life.

- "I didn't do enough today."

- "I'm not productive enough."

- "I'll relax when things are more stable."

Scarcity is sneaky because it sounds sensible. It convinces us that we'll feel fulfilled *after* we've achieved, earned, fixed, or improved something. But the finish line keeps moving. Each time we arrive, our mind shifts the goalposts a little further ahead.

Gratitude interrupts that chase. It invites you to pause and say, *What if this moment is already enough to hold some good?*

That doesn't mean giving up ambition or settling for less. It simply means learning to appreciate what's here, instead of postponing peace until life behaves perfectly.

Psychologist Robert Emmons — one of the leading researchers on gratitude — puts it this way:

"Gratitude blocks toxic emotions like envy, resentment, and regret, which can destroy our happiness. It helps us savour positive experiences, cope with stress, and build stronger relationships."

When gratitude shifts your focus from what's missing to what's present, your emotional landscape changes. You move from scanning for danger to scanning for delight. You become more resilient not because life is easier, but because your mind no longer amplifies every difficulty into catastrophe.

This shift is subtle at first, almost invisible. But as it builds, the difference is profound. You stop feeling like life is something to be survived and start feeling that it's something you're actually *in*.

The Quiet Power of Perspective

Perspective is everything. The same event — a delayed train, a cancelled plan, a rainy day — can be seen as either inconvenience or opportunity, depending on where you place your attention.

When you're living on autopilot, your brain tends to interpret neutral events negatively. A slow queue becomes a waste of time. A quiet weekend feels like boredom. Gratitude flips that pattern. It trains your brain to interpret the same situations through a wider lens:

"This delay gives me a moment to breathe."
"This quiet weekend is a chance to recharge."

The external situation hasn't changed — but your internal chemistry has. That's the gratitude shift in action.

Every reframed thought sends new signals through your brain's neural pathways. The more often you choose appreciation, the stronger those pathways become, until gratitude becomes less an effort and more a reflex.

And that's when life begins to feel lighter — not because it's perfect, but because *you've stopped waiting for it to be*.

The Science of Reframing

If gratitude were simply a matter of saying "thank you" more often, it wouldn't have such remarkable effects. What makes gratitude powerful is that it changes the way the brain processes and prioritises information.

Human beings are wired with what psychologists call a **negativity bias** — an ancient survival system designed to keep us safe. Our brains give far more attention to potential threats than to neutral or pleasant experiences. It's why you might forget ten compliments but remember one piece of criticism all week.

This bias helped our ancestors survive in dangerous environments, but in modern life, it can keep us trapped in chronic vigilance. Even on calm days, the mind scans for what might go wrong, what's unfinished, or what needs improvement. Gratitude gently retrains this system.

When you consciously notice something positive — even briefly — your brain releases a small pulse of dopamine, the neurotransmitter linked with motivation and reward. That hit of "feel-good" chemistry reinforces the act of noticing itself, making you more likely to do it again. Over time, gratitude builds new neural pathways that favour appreciation over anxiety.

Neuroscientists have observed this effect in real time. Functional MRI scans show that when people reflect on things they're grateful for, the **prefrontal cortex** and **anterior cingulate cortex** — regions associated with emotion regulation and moral reasoning — become more active. Meanwhile, the **amygdala**, which governs fear and reactivity, shows reduced activity.

In simpler terms: gratitude literally calms the alarm system in your brain. It shifts your inner state from defence to openness.

Reframing in Action

Reframing is the process of consciously choosing a different interpretation of an event or feeling. Gratitude is one of the most effective ways to practise it, because it doesn't require denial — only inclusion.

Instead of "This is terrible," gratitude says, "This is difficult, *and* I can still find something steady here."
Instead of "I failed," it says, "I learned."
Instead of "Nothing goes my way," it whispers, "This moment might still hold something I need."

This isn't wishful thinking. It's the psychology of balance.

Cognitive-behavioural therapists often teach clients to identify and challenge automatic negative thoughts. Gratitude works in a similar way, but through emotion as much as logic. When you feel grateful, your body's stress response settles, making it easier to think clearly and reframe naturally.

The practice becomes self-sustaining: appreciation reduces tension, calm increases perspective, perspective makes gratitude easier to access. You've created a positive feedback loop in your own nervous system.

Small Shifts, Lasting Effects

Even micro-reframes can make a measurable difference. A 2021 study in *Behavioural Therapy and Research* found that people who practised daily gratitude journaling for two weeks showed a 25% increase in positive emotions and a marked decrease in repetitive worry. The key wasn't the *length* of their lists, but the *depth* of reflection — understanding *why* each thing mattered.

Another study at the University of Southern California revealed that gratitude training enhanced activity in the hypothalamus — the part of the brain that regulates sleep, metabolism, and stress hormones. In other words, appreciation doesn't just feel good emotionally; it's physically restorative.

Your brain doesn't need grand experiences to trigger this response. A moment of noticing the warmth of sunlight, a kind word, or a shared laugh can activate the same pathways. Each act of noticing teaches your nervous system that safety and satisfaction are available here, now.

The Reframing Mindset

The more you practise gratitude, the more naturally reframing begins to happen. You'll start catching yourself mid-thought and softening the language:

- "I have to" becomes "I get to."
- "This is too much" becomes "This is a lot, but I can take one step."
- "I'm behind" becomes "I'm moving at my own pace."

These small edits are subtle acts of self-compassion. They don't ignore difficulty, but they remind you that struggle isn't the whole story.

Over time, reframing turns gratitude into an instinct — a quiet internal voice that steadies you before stress can spiral. The more often you listen for that voice, the more often you'll find it's already there.

The Language of Lack vs. The Language of Enough

If you listen carefully to the way you speak — to others and to yourself — you'll start to notice how often your words lean towards *lack*.

"I should be doing more."
"I never get a break."
"I always mess things up."
"I can't relax until everything's done."

These phrases sound ordinary, even harmless, but they reveal a mental script that keeps us trapped in dissatisfaction. Words like *should*, *never*, *always*, and *can't* close our thinking; they harden our perception until every moment feels like a test we're failing.

This is what psychologists sometimes call **deficit language** — speech patterns that focus on what's missing, inadequate, or still undone. Deficit language creates tension, even when life is objectively fine. It keeps your brain tuned to shortage and pressure, always scanning for what needs fixing.

Gratitude speaks a different dialect. It uses the **language of enoughness** — softer, slower, and far kinder.
It says:
"I'm doing what I can."
"I'm grateful for this small pocket of quiet."
"I made a mistake, but I learned something from it."
"I can rest even when everything isn't finished."

Notice how these sentences open rather than close. They leave room for relief, perspective, and self-acceptance.

The difference between lack and enough isn't about ignoring problems; it's about refusing to narrate your life solely through what's missing. When you practise gratitude, you're not denying reality — you're expanding it. You're making space for both imperfection *and* appreciation to coexist.

Why Words Matter

Language shapes perception. Neuroscientists have shown that the words we use influence not only thought but also emotional tone and even body chemistry. When you describe your day as "hectic" or "disastrous," your nervous system responds accordingly, priming you for tension and alertness. When you call it "full" or "challenging but manageable," your brain receives a different signal: there's space to breathe.

In gratitude practice, words are your tools of reprogramming. Each time you phrase a thought more gently or thankfully, you're helping your brain recognise safety and sufficiency. Over time, your language literally rewires your emotional patterns.

One 2017 study from Stanford University found that reappraising events using neutral or positive language decreased amygdala activity (the part of the brain linked to fear) and increased emotional stability. Simply changing how we *talk* about our experiences can change how we *feel* about them.

This is why gratitude journaling, when done mindfully, is so effective. It isn't the list itself that matters — it's the narrative you create while writing. The words you choose form the story you live inside.

How to Shift Your Inner Dialogue

You can start tuning your language towards enoughness with a few gentle swaps:

Language of Lack	Language of Enough
"I have to."	"I get to."
"I'll be happy when..."	"I can find a small joy now."
"It's all going wrong."	"Some things are hard, but not everything."
"I'm behind."	"I'm moving at my own pace."
"It's not perfect."	"It's progress."

At first, this might feel contrived — like you're talking yourself into something. But with repetition, these phrases begin to feel natural, even comforting. They remind you that contentment isn't found in fixing everything but in noticing what's already working.

Gratitude doesn't demand that you ignore what hurts. It simply asks that you include what helps too. When you replace the harsh edges of lack with the gentle curves of enough, life begins to sound — and feel — more peaceful.

The Gentle Practice of Rephrasing

Try listening for the moments when your mind drifts into deficit language during the day. You don't need to correct every thought — just notice and soften one. If you hear yourself say, "I have so much to do," add,

"and I'm grateful I'm capable of doing it."
If you think, "Nothing's going my way," try, "This part is hard, but it's not the whole story."

Even a single amended sentence shifts the energy of your day. Over time, this becomes automatic — gratitude naturally edits your inner narration into something more balanced and true.

Your life hasn't changed; your language has. And that makes all the difference.

From Awareness to Appreciation

Awareness is the doorway; appreciation is what steps through it.

The moment you begin to notice more — the taste of your morning tea, the tone of someone's laughter, the relief of exhaling after a busy day — you create an opening. Gratitude is what fills that space. It's the natural response to truly seeing.

You can't force appreciation any more than you can force calm. It grows from noticing. Once you become aware of the small details that make life bearable or beautiful, gratitude begins to surface on its own. It doesn't arrive with fireworks; it arrives like a quiet sigh — a soft recognition that *this moment, right here, is enough.*

From Pressure to Presence

Most of us have been conditioned to live in what psychologists call *achievement mode* — the constant pursuit of the next milestone, the next improvement, the next reason to feel worthy. Gratitude invites you to step out of that mode and into *presence.*

Presence doesn't mean giving up on your goals. It means returning to yourself while you pursue them. It's the pause that reminds you that even as you move forward, there's goodness right where you stand.

When you shift from pressure to presence, life stops feeling like a race and begins to feel like a rhythm. You can still strive, but now you're doing it from a place of fullness, not lack.

The Alchemy of Attention

Attention is one of the most powerful forces you possess. Whatever you focus on expands — not because the world changes, but because your perception does. Gratitude teaches you to use that power wisely.

Each time you focus your attention on what's working, what's kind, or what's meaningful, you train your brain to create more of it. The psychologist Barbara Fredrickson calls this the **broaden-and-build effect**: positive emotions like gratitude broaden our awareness, helping us see more possibilities, connect more deeply, and build psychological resilience.

It's the opposite of the narrowing effect of stress. Where stress says "tunnel," gratitude says "horizon."

A New Way of Seeing

The world doesn't change when you start practising gratitude — but the way you see it does.
The spilled coffee, the delayed bus, the challenging meeting — they still happen. But they no longer define

your day. They become background noise rather than the whole story.

And in the foreground?
A hundred small graces you used to overlook: the warmth of a blanket, the kindness of a friend, the smell of rain, the laughter that sneaks up on you when you least expect it.

This is what gratitude does. It doesn't promise perfection. It promises perspective.

It takes the ordinary and makes it luminous.

Gratitude as Practice, Not Performance

Remember: gratitude isn't a personality trait you either have or don't. It's a skill — one that strengthens with practice and patience. You don't need to feel grateful all the time, and you don't need to impress anyone with elaborate lists. You simply need to keep noticing.

When you forget (and you will), start again.
When you're too busy, find five seconds instead of five minutes.
When you feel low, look for the smallest, most honest thing you can thank life for — a breath, a bed, a glimmer of light.

The more you return to this practice, the more it becomes who you are. Not someone pretending to be positive, but someone awake to the beauty that's already here.

Reflection & Action Prompt

Your challenge:
For the next week, choose one everyday moment —
making tea, brushing your teeth, or walking to your car
— and use it as your *awareness anchor*.
Each time you do it, pause, breathe, and find one thing
to appreciate in that moment.

It might be the warmth of the mug, the clean smell of
toothpaste, or the open sky overhead.
That's all. No lists, no pressure. Just noticing.

Because the more you notice, the more your life begins
to feel like something worth noticing.

Chapter 4 – The 5-Minute Gratitude Habit

Why Small Steps Work Best

Most people imagine transformation as a grand event — a breakthrough, a new year's resolution, a big reset. But the truth is quieter.
Real change happens in the small moments, repeated often enough that they start to reshape how you live.

That's what the five-minute habit is about: creating a daily pocket of calm that teaches your mind to notice the good automatically.

It doesn't matter when or where you do it. Morning, lunchtime, before bed — the time isn't important. What matters is *frequency*. The brain doesn't learn from intensity; it learns from repetition.

Think of it like building strength. You wouldn't go to the gym once for two hours and expect lasting results. You'd go regularly, doing small amounts that compound over time. Gratitude works exactly the same way — brief, consistent practice creates deeper wiring than occasional bursts of effort.

Psychologists call this **the consistency principle**: small, repeated behaviours shape identity more effectively than sporadic big ones. When you commit to five minutes of gratitude each day, you're not only training your brain — you're signalling to yourself, *this matters to me*. That identity shift is where the real change begins.

Five Minutes Can Change the Tone of Your Day

Five minutes might not sound like much, but the research is surprisingly strong.
A 2019 study published in *The Journal of Positive Psychology* found that even two to three minutes of focused gratitude reflection improved participants' mood and reduced anxiety throughout the day.
Another study from Berkeley's Greater Good Science Centre showed that people who spent just a few minutes each morning noting small positives reported higher satisfaction and more resilience after two weeks.

These brief check-ins act as emotional recalibration points. They interrupt mental autopilot and remind your nervous system that safety and calm still exist, even in busy or uncertain moments.

Those five minutes are a reset button — a space between stimulus and response. Instead of starting your day reacting to emails or ending it replaying stress, you consciously anchor yourself in appreciation.

Over time, these short pauses accumulate into something profound: a quieter mind, a steadier mood, and a growing sense that life feels *enough*, even when imperfect.

How to Begin the Habit

Start by choosing a consistent moment in your day that already exists — something you do without fail. That's your anchor.

It might be:

- The moment you wake up, before you check your phone.

- Sitting down with your morning coffee.

- The quiet few minutes after work before you start dinner.

- Just before bed, as you wind down.

Linking gratitude to an existing routine (what psychologists call **habit stacking**) makes it easier to remember.

For example:

"After I brush my teeth, I'll think of one thing I'm grateful for."
"After I make my first cup of tea, I'll write down one small moment that made me smile."

The cue triggers the habit automatically. Within a few weeks, you won't need reminders — your mind will start seeking those pauses naturally.

Keep It Effortless

Gratitude practice doesn't have to be formal. You can write in a journal, type a quick note on your phone, or simply think it silently. Some people prefer whispering their gratitude aloud while walking, driving, or cooking — almost like a conversation with life itself.

What matters most is *genuine attention*. A few heartfelt seconds of awareness are far more powerful than a long, distracted list.

If you prefer structure, try this simple rhythm:

1. **Name one thing you're grateful for.**

2. **Say why it matters.**

3. **Notice how it feels.**

That's it. Three steps, five minutes, a lifetime of difference.

Building Momentum (Making Gratitude Stick)

Starting a habit is one thing. Keeping it going — especially when life gets busy — is another story. Gratitude, like any practice, has an initial glow. In the first few days, you feel calmer, more aware, more connected. Then, inevitably, life crowds back in: deadlines, noise, fatigue. The notebook gathers dust.

That's normal. Every habit has a *dip*. Momentum builds when you learn how to move through that dip with gentleness instead of guilt.

The key is to remember that consistency doesn't mean perfection. It means *returning*.

Emotion Before Effort

One of the simplest ways to strengthen a habit is to make it emotionally rewarding. Your brain is wired to repeat what feels good. Each time you complete your gratitude practice, take a second to notice how your body feels.

Do you feel lighter? Calmer? A little more grounded? That moment of satisfaction is your built-in reinforcement loop. When you consciously register that feeling, your brain releases a small dose of dopamine, which cements the behaviour in memory.

Psychologist Judson Brewer, who studies habit formation at Brown University, calls this *reward-based learning*. You're not forcing discipline; you're creating pleasure around the practice itself. The next time your mind hesitates — *I don't have time for this today* — the memory of that emotional lift makes it easier to begin again.

The "Start Small" Strategy

Gratitude only sticks when it feels realistic.
If five minutes feels too long, start with one. If writing feels tedious, speak it aloud. Lowering the bar doesn't weaken the habit; it protects it. The smaller and easier it feels, the more likely you are to keep going.

And here's the lovely paradox: once you begin, momentum often carries you further than planned. You might sit down for one minute and find yourself writing three. The hardest part of any habit is *starting*; once you begin, your brain's natural completion drive kicks in.

So, instead of aiming for perfect consistency, aim for **easy beginnings**.

Anchor, Reward, Repeat

Every lasting habit follows the same pattern:
Cue → Action → Reward.

For gratitude, your *cue* might be your morning coffee, your commute, or brushing your teeth. The *action* is your five-minute reflection. The *reward* is that subtle sense of calm or perspective you feel afterwards.

The more often you repeat the full loop, the stronger it becomes. After a few weeks, you won't need to think about it — your brain will associate the cue (say, the sound of the kettle boiling) with a micro-moment of stillness and appreciation.

This is where the practice begins to run on its own energy — a gentle momentum that sustains itself.

Overcoming Resistance

Everyone hits days when gratitude feels impossible — when you're too tired, frustrated, or simply uninspired. The trick isn't to push through with fake positivity; it's to adapt.

On those days, try what I call a **neutral gratitude**: Instead of forcing "I'm grateful for everything," go simpler.
"I'm grateful for this cup of tea."
"I'm grateful that today is over."
"I'm grateful for my bed."

It doesn't have to be profound. The aim is simply to stay connected to *some* sense of steadiness. Even neutral gratitude keeps your neural pathways active — and on difficult days, that's enough.

Celebrate Small Wins

Momentum grows through recognition.
Each time you show up for your five-minute habit, even briefly, acknowledge it. You might say quietly, *I kept my promise to myself today.* That acknowledgement reinforces self-trust — the foundation of any sustainable habit.

You can even track progress visually if it motivates you: a tick in a calendar box, a tally mark in a notebook, a reminder in your phone. The goal isn't productivity; it's visibility — a gentle reminder that you're cultivating something valuable, one small act at a time.

Let the Habit Evolve

Gratitude isn't static. What begins as a few written lines might one day expand into mindful walking, deeper journaling, or spontaneous expressions of thanks to others. Let the habit evolve naturally.

The five-minute practice isn't a cage; it's a gateway. Once gratitude has a place in your daily rhythm, it tends to spread — into how you speak, notice, and respond. You'll find yourself saying "thank you" more often, pausing before reacting, or seeing beauty where you didn't before.

That's when you know the practice has taken root — not because you're ticking boxes, but because gratitude has quietly become your way of seeing.

When Gratitude Feels Flat (Reconnecting with Meaning)

It happens to everyone. You start with good intentions — the notebook, the quiet moment, the list of three things. At first, it feels grounding. Then one day, you sit down to write and feel... nothing. The words look the same, but they don't land. The spark's gone.

You're not failing. You're evolving.

When gratitude feels flat, it's usually a sign that your mind has adapted — and that's actually progress. The early buzz fades because your brain has grown familiar with the practice. You're no longer getting the "novelty effect" of doing something new. This is the moment to go deeper, not give up.

Depth Over Quantity

If your gratitude list has become repetitive, try slowing it down. Instead of writing ten quick items, focus on one or two and explore *why* they matter.

For example:
Instead of "I'm grateful for my morning coffee," you might write,
"I'm grateful for my morning coffee because it marks the start of quiet before the day begins. It's the warmth in my hands, the smell that reminds me to breathe, the ritual that says, 'you're here.'"

That extra reflection changes everything. You're no longer collecting words; you're feeling the experience. The emotional depth reignites the brain's reward system, restoring that sense of calm and appreciation.

Change the Medium

If journaling feels stale, change how you express gratitude. Speak it aloud. Record a voice note. Take a photo of something that brings you joy. Text someone to thank them. Gratitude doesn't need to stay on paper — it's meant to move through you.

When you change the form, you wake the practice up. Each new channel of expression re-engages your senses, making the experience more embodied. You move from *thinking* about gratitude to *feeling* it again.

Expand the Focus

Sometimes gratitude loses spark because it's become self-contained — always focused on *your* day, *your* comforts, *your* perspective. Try turning the lens outward. Notice kindness in others, beauty in nature, or even the resilience of strangers.

You could reflect on:

- Someone else's effort that made your day smoother.

- The unseen people behind ordinary comforts — the farmer who grew your food, the driver who delivered your parcel, the teacher who shaped your child's morning.

This outward shift restores a sense of connection — reminding you that gratitude isn't just a personal mood-booster, it's a social glue. It quietly connects you to the web of life around you.

Honest Gratitude

When you're low, gratitude can feel forced. The mind rebels: *How can I be thankful when I'm exhausted, lonely, or anxious?*

In those moments, aim for honesty rather than enthusiasm.
You might write, "I'm grateful that I'm trying, even though I feel stuck."
Or, "I'm grateful that I made it through today, even if nothing felt easy."

That kind of honesty is powerful. It blends gratitude with self-compassion — a combination that psychologists say strengthens emotional resilience far more than surface-level positivity.

Real gratitude isn't about pretending you're fine. It's about recognising that even in pain, there's still some small thread of okayness — a reason to keep going.

Rediscover the Sensory

If words aren't working, return to your senses.
Sit quietly and ask:
What can I see right now that's beautiful?
What can I hear that's soothing?
What can I feel that's comforting?

Maybe it's the hum of the fridge, the rhythm of your breathing, or the weight of your pet's head on your lap. These sensory anchors pull you back into the present, where gratitude naturally lives. You can't *think* your way to appreciation — you have to *feel* your way there.

It's Not About the List

Most importantly, remember: gratitude isn't a checklist. It's a relationship. Some days it flows; other days it flickers. The value isn't in what you record but in the awareness you return to, even briefly.

A flat practice doesn't mean it's failing. It means it's settling in — moving from an activity you *do* to a mindset you *carry.*

If you stay with it — gently, without pressure — that sense of meaning will return, deeper and steadier than before.

Reflection & Action Prompt

Your challenge:
For the next few days, choose *one* thing you're grateful for and spend your whole five-minute practice exploring it in detail.

Ask yourself:

- Why does this matter to me?

- What would life feel like without it?

- What sensations or emotions arise when I think of it?

By focusing on quality over quantity, you'll rediscover the quiet richness that makes gratitude come alive again.

Chapter 5 – Gratitude on the Hard Days

When Gratitude Feels Impossible

There are days when gratitude feels out of reach. Days when you wake up heavy, when the world feels too sharp or too loud, and the idea of writing a list of blessings seems almost offensive.

You know those days. The ones when the kettle boils but you forget to pour the water. When you stare at your phone and can't process the words. When you feel tired in a way that sleep can't touch.

In those moments, it's easy to think, *I can't do gratitude right now. I'll come back to it when things are better.*

But here's the truth: gratitude isn't meant only for the good days. It was made for the hard ones.

Gratitude isn't the denial of pain — it's the discovery of stillness within it. It's the quiet act of saying, *even here, something small still holds me.*

Pain and Possibility Can Coexist

One of the biggest misconceptions about gratitude is that it cancels out suffering. It doesn't. What it does is *create space around it.*

You can be sad and still grateful. You can feel anxious and still appreciate a moment of calm. You can be grieving and still notice a ray of sunlight on the floor.

In fact, psychologists have found that gratitude during hardship can significantly buffer emotional distress. In a 2018 study on resilience, researchers discovered that participants who kept a simple daily gratitude log during periods of high stress reported lower levels of depression and more stable mood. Gratitude didn't erase their pain — but it changed their relationship to it.

That's the power of dual awareness: the ability to hold two truths at once — *this hurts, and there is still good here.*

When you practise gratitude on the hard days, you're not pretending everything is fine. You're simply reminding your nervous system that safety and goodness still exist alongside difficulty.

This balance helps prevent the brain from slipping fully into threat mode, where all attention narrows to what's wrong. Gratitude gently widens that tunnel, letting in just enough light to keep you steady.

Micro-Gratitude in the Storm

When life feels overwhelming, big gratitude practices are often too much. That's when **micro-gratitude** becomes your anchor — noticing the smallest, most tangible things that don't demand effort or performance.

It might sound like:

- "I'm grateful for this cup of tea."

- "I'm grateful that I'm breathing."

- "I'm grateful the day is nearly over."

- "I'm grateful for the kindness of the nurse, the friend, the stranger."

Tiny acknowledgements like these matter. They aren't meant to lift you instantly into joy — they're meant to stop you from sinking further into despair.

On the darkest days, gratitude isn't a mood booster; it's a lifeline.

Letting Go of Perfection

Hard days can also reveal another trap: the belief that gratitude has to look a certain way. You might think, *I should write something deep. I should feel more thankful.*

But forced gratitude backfires. It becomes another pressure, another "should."

Real gratitude doesn't demand emotion; it only asks for attention. You don't need to *feel* grateful to *be* grateful. The feeling often follows the noticing, not the other way around.

So if all you can manage is one word — "sunlight," "warmth," "tea," "breath" — let that be enough.

Sometimes gratitude is simply the act of showing up.

How the Body Carries You

On difficult days, try shifting your focus from thoughts to sensations. Gratitude for the body is one of the most grounding practices there is — especially when your mind is spinning.

Notice what your body is doing for you, quietly, without asking. Your lungs still breathing. Your heart still beating. Your feet still carrying you, even when you don't feel like moving.

When you place attention there, something softens. The body reminds you that life continues to move through you, even when you feel stuck. That in itself is worth a moment of thanks.

A Gentle Ritual for Rough Days

When gratitude feels far away, here's a five-step "hard day" ritual to bring you back:

1. **Pause.** Stop what you're doing. Take one slow breath in and one slow breath out.

2. **Acknowledge.** Name what's hard — honestly, without judgement. ("Today feels heavy.")

3. **Anchor.** Find one neutral thing that's okay right now. It could be your chair, the weather, or the sound of your pet snoring nearby.

4. **Appreciate.** Offer a quiet thank you for that one thing. ("I'm glad for this bit of steadiness.")

5. **Rest.** Don't chase the feeling. Let it land gently, even if it lasts just a few seconds.

That's it. No journaling, no lists, no rules. Just a simple act of remembering that goodness hasn't disappeared — it's just smaller and quieter right now.

The Strength in Softness

Practising gratitude on the hard days is a kind of courage. It's choosing softness in a world that often rewards hardness. It's saying, "I refuse to let pain have the final word."

Gratitude doesn't erase grief or struggle — it coexists with them. It steadies your hands enough to keep holding on. And sometimes, that's all you need to get through.

Reflection & Action Prompt

Your challenge:
On your next hard day, pause for one minute.
Without forcing cheerfulness, name *one* thing that is still holding you — a person, a sound, a sensation, a memory.
Write it down or whisper it aloud.

That single act is enough. Gratitude isn't always loud or shining; sometimes, it's just the quiet strength that keeps you standing.

Chapter 6 – Relationships and the Ripple Effect

The Ripple Effect of Gratitude

When you start to practise gratitude regularly, something interesting happens: it doesn't stay contained within you. It begins to spill out — softening the way you speak, listen, and respond.

Gratitude isn't only a private feeling; it's a relational one. Every "thank you," every quiet moment of appreciation, sends a ripple through your connections with others. Those ripples can change the atmosphere of a room, a conversation, even a relationship that's grown tense or distant.

Psychologists have found that expressing gratitude strengthens social bonds in measurable ways. In one landmark study at the University of California, researchers observed that when people received genuine thanks, their brains showed increased activation in areas linked with trust and empathy. The simple act of being appreciated made them more likely to cooperate, to forgive, and to pass kindness on.

Gratitude, in other words, is contagious — but in the best possible way.

When you thank someone sincerely, you're not just acknowledging what they did; you're acknowledging *them*. You're saying, "I see you. What you do matters." And in a world where so many people feel unseen, that recognition can be quietly healing.

Why Relationships Thrive on Appreciation

Think for a moment about the last time someone truly thanked you — not out of politeness, but from the heart. Maybe they noticed a small effort you made or told you the difference you'd made to their day.

Didn't it shift something inside you?
Maybe you stood a little taller, smiled without realising, or felt a wave of warmth spread through your chest. That's oxytocin — the "connection hormone" — being released. It's the same chemical that strengthens bonding between parents and infants, friends, and partners.

Every expression of gratitude becomes a small dose of relational glue. It tells both people, *this is safe, this is kind, this is worth continuing.*

Over time, gratitude builds a shared emotional bank account — a reservoir of goodwill that helps relationships weather conflict or misunderstanding. When life feels pressured and small irritations arise, that bank balance of appreciation cushions the impact.

Couples' therapist John Gottman famously found that thriving relationships maintain roughly a **5:1 ratio** of positive to negative interactions — five moments of kindness, humour, or appreciation for every criticism or complaint. Gratitude is one of the simplest ways to build that positive ratio without forcing anything.

The Everyday Ripple

The ripple effect doesn't stop with close relationships. Gratitude changes the small, passing connections too — the brief smile exchanged with a neighbour, the friendly word to a cashier, the moment of patience in traffic.

When you approach daily life with a grateful mindset, you unconsciously communicate it through tone, body language, and attention. People feel safer around you. Interactions that might have been purely transactional become a little more human.

It's not magic; it's presence. When you're aware of what's good, you show up differently — slower to judge, quicker to appreciate. Those micro-moments accumulate, turning ordinary days into networks of quiet kindness.

This is gratitude at its most expansive: not a list in a notebook, but a way of being that brightens every relationship it touches.

Seeing People Clearly Again

One of the quiet tragedies of modern life is how easily we stop *seeing* the people closest to us.

Familiarity, for all its comfort, has a numbing effect. You stop noticing the little things your partner does — the way they make your tea, or always check the doors before bed. You forget to thank your colleague who always smooths the day's chaos behind the scenes. You overlook the friend who listens without judgment, or the neighbour who waves every morning.

It's not unkindness — it's inattention. Life moves fast, and the brain, ever efficient, filters out what feels routine. What once felt precious becomes background noise.

But gratitude reverses that drift.

When you practise gratitude, you start to *see* people again — their gestures, their efforts, their presence. Your focus shifts from what's missing or frustrating to what's quietly sustaining. The small acts you once overlooked begin to glow with significance.

The Psychology of Familiarity Blindness

Psychologists sometimes call this *hedonic adaptation* — the tendency to get used to good things until they stop registering. The human mind adjusts quickly to comfort and kindness, treating them as the new normal. Gratitude disrupts that adaptation by reintroducing conscious attention.

When you pause to appreciate what someone contributes — however small — you reactivate your brain's reward pathways. The act of noticing refreshes your emotional connection to them. It's like polishing the lens through which you view the relationship; suddenly, what looked dull shines again.

In studies of long-term couples, researchers found that expressing regular gratitude was one of the strongest predictors of relationship satisfaction — more than shared hobbies, communication styles, or even conflict resolution skills. Why? Because gratitude keeps the mind alert to goodness, even when routine sets in.

When you regularly think, *I'm lucky to have them,* you automatically start treating that person as if they matter — and they feel it.

From Expectation to Appreciation

Expectations are often the quiet thieves of joy. The more we expect, the less we appreciate.

When you expect your partner to cook dinner, your colleague to stay late, or your parent to check in, their effort goes unnoticed. But when you *appreciate* it — even when it's ordinary — you shift the emotional tone completely.

Appreciation says, "I don't take you for granted."
It turns the familiar into something special again.

This doesn't mean you have to shower people with constant praise. It simply means taking a moment to *register* the small kindnesses — a message sent, a meal shared, a task done quietly in the background.

Each recognition strengthens the invisible bridge between you.

A Simple Practice to See Others Again

Here's a gentle exercise you can try tonight:

Think of one person you see often — at home, work, or in your community.
Ask yourself:

- What's one small thing they do that makes life easier or lighter?

- When was the last time I thanked them for it — even silently?

Then, take a moment to feel that appreciation. You don't have to say anything yet; just notice the feeling.

That small act of awareness is enough to shift how you interact with them tomorrow.

Gratitude clears the fog of familiarity. It brings the people we love — and even the people we barely notice — back into focus.

Gratitude Without People-Pleasing

Gratitude is powerful, but like any strength, it can tilt out of balance.

Many of us were raised to equate politeness with self-sacrifice — to say yes when we mean no, to thank people excessively, or to apologise for taking up space. Over time, that conditioning turns gratitude from a warm connection into a quiet performance.

You end up thanking people for things you didn't actually want, or expressing appreciation out of fear rather than truth. The words sound kind, but they leave a hollow feeling — as though you've given away a little piece of yourself.

This isn't real gratitude. It's people-pleasing in disguise.

The Difference Between Gratitude and Compliance

Healthy gratitude grows from choice, not obligation. People-pleasing, on the other hand, grows from anxiety — a fear that if you stop pleasing others, love or approval will disappear.

The distinction lies in *where it comes from inside you.*

- **Gratitude** says: "I appreciate this because it adds value to my life or reflects kindness."

- **People-pleasing** says: "I'll pretend to appreciate this so no one's upset with me."

One expands your confidence and connection; the other quietly drains it.

Real gratitude comes from agency — you decide what you're thankful for, and how to express it. That freedom gives your words authenticity. People can feel the difference.

How to Spot the Difference in Yourself

A few gentle questions can help you tell whether your gratitude is genuine or people-pleasing:

- Do I feel lighter after expressing it, or slightly resentful?

- Am I saying "thank you" because I mean it, or because I'm uncomfortable with silence?

- Does my gratitude include me — or erase me?

If your expression of thanks feels like a transaction — something you owe rather than something you give freely — it's worth pausing. True gratitude never asks you to shrink.

Balancing Kindness and Boundaries

Gratitude and boundaries are not opposites; they reinforce each other.
You can thank someone and still say no.
You can appreciate help without agreeing to more than you can give.
You can express warmth without surrendering your limits.

For example:

"Thank you so much for thinking of me — I really appreciate it. I'm not able to take that on right now, but I'm grateful you asked."

That kind of response carries clarity and kindness at once. It keeps the connection intact without crossing your own edges.

Gratitude doesn't require self-sacrifice; it simply invites honesty.

Self-Gratitude: The Missing Piece

It's impossible to practise genuine gratitude toward others if you never offer any to yourself.
People-pleasers often find it easier to praise others than to acknowledge their own effort. But appreciation that flows only outward eventually runs dry.

Try this small rebalancing act:
Each time you thank someone else, thank yourself for something too.
"I'm grateful she made time for me — and I'm grateful I reached out."
"I'm thankful he cooked dinner — and thankful I made space to rest."

When gratitude includes you, it becomes a circle instead of a drain.

The Energy of Authentic Appreciation

You can feel it when gratitude is real — it lands differently. It's grounded, calm, steady. There's no pressure, no subtle pull for approval. It's simply a shared recognition: *this mattered, and I see it.*

That kind of gratitude nourishes both people. It deepens respect rather than dependency.

As you continue practising, notice not only who you're grateful for but *how* you express it. When it comes from truth, gratitude strengthens connection. When it comes from fear, it weakens it.

Learning that difference is part of the reset — the shift from performing kindness to living it.

Everyday Expressions of Thanks

Gratitude is most powerful when it leaves your head and enters the world.
It doesn't have to be poetic or profound — just real. A simple, sincere "thank you" offered at the right moment can soften tension, spark warmth, or even change the course of someone's day.

But because we often assume people "already know" we appreciate them, we forget to say it aloud. Gratitude left unspoken helps no one — it's like writing a letter and never posting it.

Small Words, Big Impact

Psychologists studying gratitude expression have found something remarkable: *it matters far more than we think it does.*
In one study at the University of Chicago, participants who wrote short thank-you notes expected the recipients to feel mildly pleased. In reality, most

recipients reported feeling deeply moved — and often kept the note for months afterwards.

People underestimate how powerful simple gratitude can be. What feels ordinary to you might be extraordinary to someone who rarely hears appreciation.

You don't need grand speeches or fancy wording. A few honest sentences are enough:

"I just wanted to say thank you for always listening — it makes a big difference."
"I really appreciated your patience with me today."
"You probably don't realise how much your calm presence helps."

Those moments ripple far beyond the words themselves. They leave people feeling valued, seen, and energised — and that energy tends to flow back to you.

Everyday Ways to Express Gratitude

Here are a few easy, natural ways to weave gratitude into your day:

- **Say it in real time.** When someone helps or supports you — even in small ways — say thank you right then. Don't save it for later.

- **Write it down.** A short message, card, or email takes two minutes but can lift someone's whole week.

- **Be specific.** Instead of "Thanks for everything," try "Thank you for remembering the details — it means a lot." Specificity shows attention, which deepens sincerity.

- **Show it, don't just say it.** Make someone a cup of tea, share a compliment, give them time off from a shared task. Actions often carry gratitude more clearly than words.

- **Practice "quiet thanks."** Sometimes the best gratitude is unspoken — a gentle smile, eye contact, or a slower tone that communicates appreciation without fanfare.

The key is to let gratitude sound like *you*. Whether you're reserved or expressive, formal or casual, your authentic tone is always enough.

Gratitude at Home, Work, and Beyond

Different settings call for different forms of appreciation:

- **At home**, it might be a whispered "thank you for doing that" at the sink, or a quick note tucked into someone's bag.

- **At work**, it could be a short message recognising a colleague's effort — "You handled that so calmly; it helped everyone."

- **In friendships**, it might be a simple text: "I really appreciate you being in my life."

- **In public**, even eye contact and a kind word to a stranger can create a moment of connection that ripples outward.

These gestures seem small, but collectively, they change the emotional climate around you. You'll start to notice that people relax more easily, smile more readily, and respond in kind. Gratitude subtly shifts how others experience being near you — and how you experience them.

Making Gratitude a Shared Language

When gratitude becomes part of how you communicate, relationships feel lighter and safer. People stop guessing whether they're valued; they can *feel* it.

Over time, you'll find that your appreciation encourages others to reciprocate — not out of duty, but naturally. You create what psychologists call a *positive feedback loop*: the more appreciation is expressed, the more kindness and cooperation grow.

In that sense, gratitude isn't only personal development; it's community building. It transforms relationships from transactional to meaningful.

A Small Daily Practice

Try this: once a day, choose one person to acknowledge — silently or aloud.
You might thank your child for their curiosity, your colleague for their effort, or a stranger for a simple act of courtesy.

If you can, be specific: what did they do, and how did it help you?

Over time, this becomes second nature — not another task, but a way of seeing. Gratitude spoken aloud becomes a language of connection that everyone understands.

Repairing and Reconnecting

Even the closest relationships sometimes fray. Words are spoken in frustration, misunderstandings build up, or silence grows heavy between two people who used to understand each other easily.

In those moments, gratitude might not be the first thing that comes to mind. You might feel too angry, too disappointed, or too tired to look for anything good. And yet, gratitude — in its simplest, most honest form — can be one of the gentlest ways to begin repairing the threads.

Gratitude doesn't erase what went wrong. It simply opens a door. It reminds both people that beyond the tension, there is still something shared and worth preserving.

When Conflict Hardens the Heart

When conflict arises, our brains automatically shift into *defensive mode*. The amygdala fires up, preparing us to protect, justify, or withdraw. In this state, we focus almost exclusively on threat and blame. The other person becomes "the problem," and empathy fades from view.

Gratitude interrupts that pattern. Even a small moment of appreciation — silently thinking, *They're trying their best* or *I do care about them* — signals safety to the nervous system. It tells your body, *This person is not my enemy.*

Once that message lands, the brain softens. The prefrontal cortex, which governs empathy and reason, comes back online. You can listen again. You can breathe again. You can see the person, not just the argument.

It's a physiological reset — and one that can make reconciliation possible.

Starting Small: The Power of One Kind Word

Repair rarely begins with grand gestures. It starts with one small moment of kindness — a genuine thank you for something still good.

You might say:

"I know we've been distant, but I really appreciate that you kept reaching out."
"Thank you for still showing up — I know it hasn't been easy."
"I just want you to know I value what we had, and I'd like to find our rhythm again."

These words don't ignore pain; they acknowledge it while gently affirming care. They shift the focus from blame to possibility. Gratitude works like a bridge — small, steady, and built plank by plank through honesty and patience.

Acknowledgement Without Excusing

It's important to remember that gratitude is not a shortcut to forgiveness, nor does it mean excusing harmful behaviour.

Sometimes the most powerful use of gratitude in a damaged relationship is *internal*: finding appreciation for what you've learned, or for the strength you've gained.

You might not be ready to thank the person — and that's fine. Gratitude can still exist quietly within you, helping you close the emotional loop so pain doesn't harden into bitterness.

True gratitude doesn't minimise what happened; it simply adds balance. It lets you say, *This hurt, and I'm still capable of seeing something worthwhile.*

Rebuilding Trust Through Appreciation

When both people are willing, gratitude can actively rebuild trust. Expressing appreciation — even for small steps — tells the other person that their effort is seen.

In therapy, couples are often encouraged to notice and thank each other for everyday acts of goodwill: showing up on time, speaking calmly, listening without interrupting. These may seem insignificant, but they quietly rewire the emotional tone of the relationship.

Each act of gratitude becomes a signal: *You matter. I notice you trying.*

That steady reinforcement helps thaw old patterns of defensiveness and fear. Over time, trust isn't rebuilt through promises — it's rebuilt through appreciation, layer by layer.

When Gratitude Becomes Closure

Sometimes, gratitude is the final step — not to reconnect, but to let go.
You might never reconcile with someone, but you can still reach a point where gratitude helps you release resentment.

You can be grateful for what that person once gave you, or for the lessons learned through difficulty. This doesn't justify their actions — it simply frees your energy from the grip of anger.

As writer Melody Beattie said, "Gratitude turns what we have into enough — and sometimes, what we had into peace."

That quiet acceptance is its own form of healing.

A Simple Exercise for Reconnection

If there's someone you'd like to reconnect with, try this gentle practice:

1. Write down three things you once appreciated about them — memories, qualities, or moments that still feel real.

2. Sit with those feelings for a minute. Notice how your body responds.

3. If it feels right, express one of those things to them — in a message, a conversation, or even a silent wish.

You don't need to fix everything. Gratitude's strength lies in its simplicity — one soft light in the dark is enough to begin seeing the way forward again.

Reflection & Action Prompt

Your challenge:
Over the next few days, choose *one person* in your life to consciously appreciate — someone you may have overlooked lately, or whose efforts you've quietly come to rely on.

It could be your partner, a colleague, a friend, a neighbour, or even a stranger who brightens your day in small ways.

Then, follow these simple steps:

1. **Notice** what they bring to your life — not in grand gestures, but in everyday ways.
    Perhaps it's their calm presence, their humour, their consistency, or the way they make ordinary moments easier.

2. **Acknowledge it — aloud or in writing.**
    You might say something as simple as:

"I realised I never thank you for how much you do — and I really should."
Or send a short message:
"Just wanted to say I appreciate you. You make things lighter."

3. **Observe how it feels.**
    Notice the small lift in your mood, the softening in their response, or the warmth that lingers between you afterwards.

4. **Repeat it — once a day if you can.**
    Gratitude expressed regularly becomes a thread that weaves strength and tenderness through every relationship you touch.

Gratitude isn't about performing niceness; it's about *seeing clearly.*
When you start looking for what's good in the people around you — and let them know you see it — you quietly change the atmosphere of your life.

Kindness feels easier. Communication feels safer. Connection feels alive again.

And that's the quiet miracle of gratitude: the more you give it away, the more it comes back to you.

Chapter 7 – Declutter Your Mental Space

The Cluttered Mind — How Overload Dulls Gratitude

Most of us know what it's like to live in physical clutter — drawers that won't close, overflowing inboxes, piles of "I'll sort it later." But there's another kind of clutter that's harder to see and even harder to clear: *mental clutter.*

It's the constant hum of unfinished thoughts and quiet worries. The running list of things you should do, say, fix, check, delete, reply to, and remember. It's the background noise that fills your head before your feet even hit the floor in the morning.

You wake up already full — not of energy, but of thoughts.

Over time, that internal busyness creates a kind of fog. You may function perfectly well on the surface — working, caring, achieving — but beneath it, your mind feels crowded and tired. Gratitude, in contrast, needs space to breathe. It thrives in stillness, in noticing, in pause. And when your head is full of static, those moments of quiet appreciation can't get through.

The Hidden Weight of "Too Much"

Modern life rewards speed and multitasking. We praise productivity, but rarely presence. We scroll while we eat, think while we walk, and answer emails between breaths. Our minds rarely stop consuming information.

The result is mental overload — what psychologists call *cognitive clutter*. When too many thoughts compete for attention, your brain struggles to filter what's important. That's why you forget what you were saying mid-sentence, or reread the same line three times without processing it.

It's also why gratitude feels harder on busy days. Appreciation depends on attention — and attention is finite. If your mind is overflowing, you simply can't notice the small moments that give life its richness.

Gratitude isn't missing; it's buried.

When Awareness Turns Into Noise

You might think constant awareness of everything — news, messages, notifications, updates — makes you informed. But often, it just fills your head with clutter that drowns out what truly matters.

This mental noise fuels stress and comparison. You see other people's highlight reels and feel you're falling behind. You check your phone for comfort and come away more restless than before. Each small distraction chips away at your capacity for stillness.

And yet, stillness is exactly where gratitude lives.

Gratitude is about focus — the ability to see clearly what's already good. But if your attention is fragmented, even beauty becomes invisible. You might pass a blooming tree or share a laugh with a loved one, but your mind is somewhere else — replaying an email or scrolling headlines.

Over time, you stop *feeling* your own life. It rushes by like scenery outside a window you've forgotten to look through.

Gratitude as Mental Minimalism

Think of gratitude as a kind of **mental decluttering**. It doesn't ask you to empty your mind completely — just to sort through the noise and make room for what matters.

When you pause to name what you're grateful for, you're effectively filtering your thoughts. You're saying, *This stays. The rest can wait.*

Each moment of appreciation acts like a mental clear-out — releasing tension, quieting the mental chatter, and refocusing your awareness on the simple, solid things that bring calm.

It's mindfulness in motion — not a blank mind, but a tidy one.

Mental Minimalism — Focusing on What Adds Value

When your mind feels crowded, it's easy to assume you need more motivation, more time, or more organisation. But often, what you really need is *less*.

Less noise.
Less comparison.
Less mental clutter disguised as productivity.

The brain, like a room, needs space to function well. If you keep piling in thoughts and obligations without clearing any out, everything begins to blur. You lose sight of what's meaningful beneath the mess.

That's where *mental minimalism* comes in — the practice of keeping only what adds value to your inner world. And gratitude is its simplest tool.

Gratitude as a Filter

Each time you pause to notice what's good, you're practising discernment. You're choosing to focus on something that enriches you instead of drains you.

That simple shift — *What matters most right now?* — is the heart of mental minimalism.

You can think of gratitude as a filter through which all your thoughts pass. It doesn't deny challenges, but it helps you separate the essential from the excessive.

For example:

- Instead of *"I have too much to do,"* gratitude says, *"I'm thankful for the opportunities that mean I'm needed."*

- Instead of *"Everyone's doing better than me,"* gratitude says, *"I'm glad I'm finding my own pace."*

- Instead of *"I should be further ahead,"* gratitude says, *"I've come further than I realise."*

It's not about ignoring reality; it's about rebalancing it. Gratitude doesn't add more to your mind — it helps you clear away what's unnecessary.

Choosing Your Focus

Every day, your attention is pulled in dozens of directions. Gratitude gently reclaims it.

When you sit down for even a few moments of stillness and reflect on what's working — a kind message, a task completed, the comfort of routine — you signal to your brain that these are the thoughts worth keeping.

Neuroscientists describe this as **selective attention**: what you focus on strengthens. Each time you choose gratitude over chaos, you reinforce the neural pathways associated with calm, clarity, and contentment. Over time, this becomes automatic — your brain starts naturally scanning for value, not clutter.

You can't control everything that enters your mental space, but you can decide what stays.

A Simple Mental Declutter

Try this quick mental minimalism exercise:

1. **Pause** for one minute.

2. **Notice** what's currently occupying your mind — the open tabs of your thoughts.

3. **Ask:** "Which of these actually matters to me right now?"

4. **Release** the rest — not forever, just for now.

5. **Anchor** your focus in one small thing you're grateful for.

This isn't a form of denial; it's emotional prioritising. You're choosing to give your attention to something nourishing instead of something depleting.

Even thirty seconds of this kind of mental tidying can bring an immediate sense of clarity — like opening a window in a crowded room.

From Overthinking to Order

When you practise gratitude regularly, it starts to impose a quiet order on your thoughts. You stop spiralling into what-ifs and begin to notice what *is*.

It's not that your responsibilities vanish; they simply take their rightful place. Instead of everything shouting at once, your mind begins to arrange itself around what feels meaningful.

Gratitude doesn't just make you calmer — it makes you *clearer*. It helps you see what deserves space and what can safely be set down.

In a world that constantly tells you to do and be more, gratitude whispers the opposite: *Simplify. Focus. Breathe.*

Digital Gratitude Detox — Creating Mental Space in a Noisy World

Modern life is full of invisible noise.
Even when the room is quiet, your phone hums with new messages, updates, opinions, and reminders — a thousand tiny voices tugging at your attention.

Each one seems harmless. But together, they fragment your focus and drain your energy. You start the day intending to check one thing and, forty minutes later, you've absorbed a dozen headlines, replied to three messages, compared your morning to someone else's highlight reel, and completely lost your sense of calm.

This constant connection gives the illusion of control, but it actually creates the opposite — *mental clutter disguised as awareness.*

Gratitude offers a gentle antidote: a way to step back, breathe, and remember what's real.

The Hidden Cost of Digital Overload

Studies show that the average person checks their phone over eighty times a day. Every glance brings a micro-spike of dopamine — a tiny burst of reward — followed by a drop. That up-and-down pattern keeps the brain seeking more stimulation, even when it feels exhausting.

It's not just time we lose; it's attention. And attention is the soil where gratitude grows.

When your focus is constantly hijacked by alerts and algorithms, there's no space left for appreciation. The mind becomes reactive rather than reflective. Gratitude fades, replaced by comparison, distraction, or low-level restlessness.

You might not feel "ungrateful," but you'll notice you're no longer *present*. And presence is where gratitude lives.

The Digital Gratitude Detox

You don't need to delete everything or disappear from the world.
The goal isn't disconnection — it's *discernment*.

A **digital gratitude detox** is simply about using technology in ways that support awareness, rather than steal it. Here's how to begin:

1. **Start with awareness.**
    For one day, simply notice how often you reach

for your phone and why. Is it boredom? Habit? Anxiety? Curiosity? Awareness alone can be transformative.

2. **Create gratitude boundaries.**
   Choose one or two "tech-free" zones in your day — perhaps breakfast, a walk, or the hour before bed. Protect these as moments for real presence.

3. **Curate what you consume.**
   Follow accounts or newsletters that inspire calm, kindness, or gratitude. Mute or unfollow those that trigger comparison, outrage, or noise. You're not being rude; you're tending to your mental garden.

4. **Replace scrolling with noticing.**
   The next time you instinctively reach for your phone, pause. Look around instead. What can you see, hear, or feel right now that's worth appreciating? The light through the window, the sound of rain, the steadiness of your own breath.

5. **End the day in gratitude, not consumption.**
   Before bed, put your phone aside and spend two minutes reflecting on what went well today — something real, something small. This tells your brain, *the day is complete,* allowing deeper rest.

Gratitude Restores Presence

When you practise small acts of digital restraint, you reclaim your most valuable resource: attention.
And with that attention, gratitude naturally returns.

You start noticing life again — not through screens, but through senses. The taste of your tea, the rhythm of conversation, the quiet hum of ordinary moments. These details are where contentment lives.

The world won't become quieter on its own. But you can choose to be.
And in that quiet, you'll rediscover a kind of clarity that no app or algorithm can give you — the peace of simply *being here*.

Reflection & Action Prompt

Your challenge:
For the next 24 hours, try a mini *Digital Gratitude Detox.*

Switch off unnecessary notifications, set one phone-free period, and spend that time noticing something real — a view, a sound, a feeling of comfort.

Then ask yourself:

"What did I notice when I wasn't looking at a screen?"

Write it down or simply hold it in mind.
That moment of awareness — that return to yourself — *is* gratitude.

Chapter 8 – Gratitude at Work and in the Mundane

Finding Meaning in Routine

Most of life isn't made up of grand moments. It's made of repetition — alarms, commutes, conversations, emails, errands, cooking, cleaning, caring, repeating.

And yet, these small, familiar rhythms are where most of our life quietly unfolds. When you learn to find gratitude within them, the ordinary becomes deeply alive again.

We often think gratitude belongs in the extraordinary: holidays, milestones, achievements. But the true power of gratitude lies in its ability to reveal beauty in what's repetitive, mundane, and easily overlooked.

The Hidden Gold in the Ordinary

When you first begin to practise gratitude, you might quickly run out of obvious things to list — family, home, food, health. Then comes the real challenge: noticing what's already embedded in your routine.

That might mean:

- The steady hum of your laptop that means work is possible.

- The colleague who always brings quiet humour to a long day.

- The first sip of coffee that starts the morning.

- The comforting familiarity of home after a tiring commute.

These details are small, but they carry stability — a sense of normality that's easy to miss until something disrupts it.

Gratitude turns these unnoticed fragments into anchors. They remind you that even in routine, there's rhythm, support, and subtle meaning.

When Routine Feels Draining

Of course, routine can also feel heavy. The repetition that brings safety can, on harder days, feel like monotony — the sense that you're stuck on a loop with no variation or recognition.

That's where gratitude shifts from being a reflection to being a choice.

You can't always change the tasks in front of you, but you can change your relationship with them. Gratitude doesn't make the work lighter — it makes it *clearer*. It reorients your attention from pressure to purpose.

Ask yourself:

- *Who benefits from this task?*

- *What does this allow me to enjoy later?*

- *What might I miss about this one day?*

Even a dull task carries meaning when you trace it to its purpose. Folding laundry becomes an act of care. Commuting becomes a bridge between worlds. Emails become connection points, however brief.

Presence Turns Work Into Worth

What gratitude really changes is *how* you pay attention.

When you give full awareness to something small — washing a dish, typing a report, serving a customer — it transforms from a chore into an act of participation. You're no longer rushing to finish; you're engaging with what *is*.

This is what psychologists call *flow*: the state where time slows and focus deepens. Gratitude helps you enter flow more easily by softening resistance. Instead of thinking, *I have to do this*, you start feeling, *I get to do this.*

And that subtle shift — from obligation to appreciation — can change how you move through every day.

Appreciation as Productivity — How Gratitude Boosts Focus and Motivation

For many people, "gratitude" and "productivity" feel like opposites. One sounds soft and emotional; the other sounds fast and efficient. But the two are quietly intertwined.

Gratitude doesn't make you less ambitious — it makes your ambition more sustainable. It doesn't slow you down; it steadies you. And steady people get more done, with less burnout and more meaning.

The Science of Productive Gratitude

Psychologists studying workplace wellbeing have repeatedly found that gratitude increases motivation and performance — not because it adds pressure, but because it strengthens connection and purpose.

In one study at the Wharton School of Business, employees who received regular expressions of thanks from their manager were 50% more productive and significantly happier in their roles. The simple act of being appreciated created a sense of belonging and meaning that no incentive scheme could match.

When you feel valued, your nervous system relaxes. Stress hormones drop, cognitive flexibility rises, and you enter what's known as an *optimal engagement state* — focused, calm, and creative. Gratitude acts as a psychological reset button, clearing emotional clutter so your mind can think clearly again.

The same applies when you offer gratitude, not just when you receive it. Thanking a colleague, acknowledging effort, or quietly noticing what's going right increases your own optimism and focus.

Gratitude turns attention away from scarcity ("I'll never get this all done") toward possibility ("Look what we've already managed"). That reframe makes momentum feel lighter, not forced.

Gratitude as a Focus Tool

Modern work culture thrives on multitasking — but the human brain doesn't. Every time you switch tasks, your mind loses efficiency, like a computer slowed by too many tabs open at once.

Gratitude can help close some of those tabs.

When you pause to recognise progress — even small wins — you anchor yourself in completion rather than chaos. That moment of appreciation signals to your brain, *This matters. This is enough for now.*

It reduces the restless urge to rush ahead, allowing deeper concentration on the next step.

You might try this mini practice:

- At the end of a meeting or task, take ten seconds to notice what went well.

- Say "thank you" aloud to a colleague, or simply in your mind.

- Then, take a slow breath before starting the next task.

That breath and acknowledgement act like punctuation in your day — a gentle full stop that clears your mind before the next sentence begins.

Gratitude and Creative Flow

Creativity and gratitude share a foundation: openness. When you're stressed or fearful, your focus narrows; your mind clings to safety and repetition. But when you're grateful, your attention broadens. You feel more curious, experimental, and optimistic — all essential ingredients for creative thinking.

In team environments, gratitude also creates psychological safety. When people feel appreciated rather than criticised, they're far more likely to share ideas, take healthy risks, and collaborate openly.

In that sense, gratitude isn't just a mood booster — it's a cultural shift. It turns workplaces from competitive to cooperative, from anxious to adaptive.

Productivity That Feels Peaceful

True productivity isn't about constant output; it's about consistent energy. Gratitude helps you maintain that steady energy by preventing mental depletion. It reminds you to pause, recognise progress, and renew motivation before fatigue sets in.

It's a quiet kind of efficiency — the kind that lasts.

When you work from appreciation rather than pressure, your effort feels less like survival and more like contribution. You stop chasing success as proof of worth and start experiencing work as participation — a way to give shape to something that matters.

That shift is what makes gratitude practical. It turns busyness into purpose, and purpose into peace.

Bringing Calm into Busy Spaces — Everyday Gratitude at Work and Home

Even when you understand the benefits of gratitude, practising it in the middle of a busy day can feel almost impossible. When the emails keep coming, deadlines loom, and people need your attention, appreciation can feel like a luxury you'll "get to later."

But that's exactly when gratitude matters most.

Gratitude doesn't ask for silence or long journalling breaks — it can live right inside the noise. It's not another task; it's a different *way of seeing* the same task.

Moments, Not Minutes

The biggest misconception about gratitude is that it requires time. It doesn't — it requires awareness.

You can practise it in small, seamless ways throughout your day:

- When you take a sip of coffee before a meeting, pause and think, *I'm glad for this warmth and quiet.*

- When a colleague sends you information on time, note, *That makes my work easier — I appreciate it.*

- When your day finally slows down, take one deep breath and notice, *I made it through.*

Each of these micro-moments rebalances your nervous system. They take seconds, but their effects linger.

Gratitude doesn't demand you stop what you're doing; it just invites you to notice while you're doing it.

Transforming the Atmosphere Around You

When you bring gratitude into your daily rhythm, you start to notice its ripple effects. People relax more easily around you. Conversations feel lighter. Even stressful situations become more cooperative, because appreciation shifts tone.

You might try starting meetings or conversations with a brief acknowledgment — "I appreciate everyone's effort on this," or "Thank you for making time today." It sounds small, but these gestures set an emotional tone that lingers.

At home, it might look like thanking someone for a routine task you often overlook — washing up, driving, tidying, or simply listening. These moments tell people: *I see you.*

When gratitude becomes part of your communication style, you stop reacting from tension and start responding from calm.

When the Day Feels Relentless

Some days, calm feels impossible. The to-do list grows instead of shrinking; interruptions pile up; patience thins. On those days, gratitude becomes an anchor rather than an ideal.

Try this reset:

1. Pause — even for thirty seconds.

2. Inhale slowly, and as you exhale, name one small thing that is still okay.

3. Feel it for a moment before moving on.

It could be something as simple as *the chair beneath me is comfortable*, or *someone smiled at me today*.

This doesn't fix the chaos, but it steadies your inner state so you can meet it with a little more grace. Gratitude doesn't erase the noise — it gives you solid ground within it.

The Link Between Gratitude and Emotional Energy

Work and home life both draw from the same emotional reservoir. When that reservoir runs dry, burnout follows. Gratitude quietly refills it.

Each moment of noticing — the effort you've made, the people supporting you, the things that function well — adds one drop back into your emotional energy tank. It's cumulative.

Over time, gratitude becomes more than a mood practice; it's emotional maintenance. It keeps your inner world tidy enough to handle the outer one with steadiness and perspective.

Reflection & Action Prompt

Your challenge:
For one full day, practise *micro-gratitude* in real time.

Whenever something goes right — or simply doesn't go wrong — pause for three seconds and acknowledge it. You don't need to write it down or say it aloud; just register it.

By evening, notice how you feel. Has the day felt any lighter? Did time feel slightly slower, or your mind slightly clearer?

These small acknowledgements create calm within chaos. And that calm, once cultivated, becomes the foundation of sustainable focus, kindness, and balance — both at work and in the everyday.

Chapter 9 – Gratitude and the Body

Appreciating the Body You Live In

Gratitude isn't only a mindset — it's an experience that lives in the body. Every breath, every step, every heartbeat is part of the story of how you move through the world. Yet for many of us, our relationship with the body is one of frustration rather than appreciation.

We judge it, compare it, push it too hard, or wish it were different. We focus on appearance instead of ability, flaws instead of function. Over time, this quiet criticism creates disconnection — the body becomes something to manage, rather than to live in.

Gratitude helps to heal that divide.

Seeing the Body Anew

Take a moment to notice everything your body does for you today without being asked. It woke you up, carried you, digested your breakfast, regulated your temperature, kept your heart beating, and your mind alert. Even as you read these words, your body is at work — absorbing oxygen, balancing hormones, repairing cells.

Most of this happens without your awareness. It's astonishing, really — a silent orchestra of activity that keeps you alive.

When you stop to recognise this, even briefly, something softens. The body shifts from being a problem to solve to a partner to thank.

Try whispering a quiet "thank you" to your body, right now.
Thank it for endurance. For holding you through tiredness. For keeping you safe enough to live, love, and notice the world.

It might feel strange at first — but gratitude, when directed inward, gradually rewires how you perceive yourself. You stop looking for what's wrong and start seeing what's working.

The Body as a Home, Not a Project

We're constantly told to "improve" our bodies — to make them smaller, stronger, more youthful, more efficient. While health and strength are worthy goals, constant striving can blur into shame.

Gratitude offers a gentler foundation for wellbeing. Instead of exercising, eating well, or resting because you dislike your body, you do it because you *appreciate* it. That shift changes everything.

When you move or rest from gratitude, your motivation comes from care, not criticism. You stop punishing your body into change and start nurturing it into balance.

Psychologists studying body image call this *body appreciation* — the ability to respect and care for your body even when you don't love every part of it. Research shows that practising body gratitude reduces anxiety, improves mood, and strengthens long-term self-esteem far more than appearance-based affirmations.

A Simple Practice: Morning Gratitude Scan

Here's a practice to begin reconnecting with your body:

1. **Before you get out of bed**, pause for 30 seconds.

2. Mentally scan your body from head to toe.

3. As you move through each area, quietly thank it for what it allows you to do.

   o "Thank you, legs, for carrying me."

   o "Thank you, hands, for creating, holding, and helping."

   o "Thank you, eyes, for letting me see the world."

You're not looking for perfection — just appreciation. Over time, this small ritual builds a foundation of respect and ease.

When you live in gratitude for your body, you begin to inhabit it more fully. Movement feels freer, rest feels deserved, and the quiet act of being alive becomes something to savour.

Your body is not an obstacle to gratitude. It's one of its purest expressions.

Movement as Gratitude — Caring for the Body Through Action

Movement is one of the simplest ways to express gratitude for being alive. Every time you stretch, walk, dance, or breathe deeply, you're reminding your body

— and your mind — that it's capable, responsive, and resilient.

Yet for many people, movement has become entangled with guilt or pressure. Exercise is often framed as something we *should* do — to burn, improve, or achieve. Gratitude gently rewrites that story.

When you move from gratitude rather than expectation, the body becomes a partner, not a project. You move because it feels good to move, not because you're trying to earn rest or approval.

Reframing Exercise as Appreciation

Try imagining every stretch or step as a small "thank you."

- A morning walk says, *thank you, legs, for strength.*

- A few shoulder rolls say, *thank you, tension, for showing me where to soften.*

- A long exhale says, *thank you, lungs, for carrying me through this day.*

This isn't sentimental — it's physiological. Movement activates the body's natural reward systems, releasing endorphins and serotonin. When paired with gratitude, those feel-good chemicals reinforce a sense of wholeness and presence.

Even slow, gentle movement — such as walking, stretching, or mindful breathing — reduces cortisol (the stress hormone) and increases vagal tone, helping the body shift into a calm, balanced state.

So when you move gratefully, you're not only strengthening muscles; you're strengthening emotional resilience.

Finding the Right Kind of Movement

Gratitude invites you to tune in to what your body *needs,* not what it "should" do.

Ask yourself:

- What kind of movement feels nurturing right now?

- Do I need energy or calm? Strength or softness?

- How can I move in a way that supports how I feel — not fights it?

Some days, that might mean a brisk walk outdoors; others, it might be a slow stretch or lying still in rest. Gratitude allows you to trust your body's signals, rather than override them with comparison or guilt.

The key is consistency, not intensity. Regular, kind movement — even five minutes at a time — signals to your body, *I value you enough to care for you.*

Walking as a Moving Meditation

Walking, in particular, is one of the most accessible gratitude practices there is. Each step becomes a rhythm of awareness — inhale, exhale, step, notice.

Try this:

- As you walk, silently name things you're grateful for in your surroundings.

- Notice textures, colours, sounds, and sensations.
- Feel the rhythm of your breath matching your pace.

You might be surprised at how quickly your mind clears. Walking in gratitude shifts you from thinking to sensing — from mental chatter to embodied presence.

It's a reminder that peace isn't always found in stillness; sometimes, it's found in motion.

Rest as Movement Too

Even stillness can be a form of grateful movement. Resting — really resting — is how the body repairs, regulates, and integrates all the effort you give it.

So when you take time to lie down, stretch gently, or breathe deeply, you're still honouring your body through action. Gratitude reframes rest from laziness to wisdom.

Movement is the body's way of saying "thank you" to life. It doesn't need to be perfect, pretty, or planned. It just needs to be intentional — a quiet acknowledgment that your body allows you to experience the world in a thousand small, miraculous ways.

Grounding Through the Senses — Coming Home to the Present Moment

The body is not only where gratitude lives — it's how we *feel* it. Every moment of appreciation passes through the senses first: the warmth of sunlight on skin, the scent of fresh coffee, the sound of rain against glass, the softness of a jumper, the taste of something comforting.

Gratitude doesn't begin in the mind; it begins in sensation. When you slow down enough to notice what the body is experiencing, you step back into the present — the only place gratitude truly exists.

The Power of Sensory Awareness

In times of stress or overthinking, the mind often drifts into the past or future — replaying, predicting, planning. The body, however, never leaves the present. That's what makes it such a powerful grounding tool.

When you consciously engage your senses, you gently anchor your awareness back to *now*.

Try this simple grounding exercise — a "five-sense gratitude reset":

1. **See** – Look around and find something pleasing to the eye. It could be the light, a plant, a colour, or a familiar object that brings comfort.

2. **Hear** – Listen for one sound that soothes or interests you — a voice, a song, a quiet hum.

3. **Touch** – Notice one texture or temperature that feels grounding: the smoothness of a mug, the warmth of a blanket, the floor under your feet.

4. **Smell** – Take in a scent that reminds you you're safe and alive — food cooking, soap, fresh air.

5. **Taste** – If possible, notice one flavour fully — tea, water, fruit, anything simple.

This exercise takes less than a minute, yet it draws your attention out of the spiral of thought and back into direct experience.

The Body's Calm Response

When you focus on the senses with gratitude, your nervous system interprets it as safety. Heart rate slows, muscles loosen, breathing deepens. The parasympathetic "rest and digest" system takes over, restoring balance.

This is why sensory gratitude practices are so effective during anxious or restless moments. You're literally teaching your body that the present moment is enough.

The more you practise this kind of sensory noticing, the quicker your body learns to self-regulate — even without conscious effort. Gratitude becomes not just a mindset, but a physical state: grounded, peaceful, and present.

Appreciation as Embodiment

To live in gratitude is to live *in* your body — to experience the world directly rather than through constant mental commentary.

Each sense becomes a pathway back to presence:

- Seeing reminds you of beauty.

- Hearing reminds you of rhythm.

- Touch reminds you of connection.

- Smell and taste remind you of life's intimacy.

Together, they form a full-body expression of gratitude — not just for what you have, but for the simple fact of *being here to feel it*.

Reflection & Action Prompt

Your challenge:
Today, choose one ordinary activity — drinking your morning tea, walking to the bus, washing your hands — and turn it into a sensory gratitude practice.

As you do it, slow down. Notice what you can see, hear, feel, smell, and taste.
Then, quietly say to yourself:

"This moment is enough."

Repeat it once or twice, and let your body register the calm that follows.

The more you practise gratitude through the senses, the more you'll find that peace isn't something you have to seek — it's something your body already knows how to return to.

Chapter 10 – Gratitude and the Future: Hope & Optimism

Hope and Vision — Seeing Tomorrow Through a Grateful Lens

Gratitude isn't only about looking back at what has gone well — it's also about looking forward with trust.

When you live with appreciation, your view of the future changes. You stop seeing it as a place filled with uncertainty and start seeing it as a space filled with possibility. Gratitude becomes a kind of lens, softening fear and sharpening hope.

We often think of hope and gratitude as separate emotions — one for what hasn't happened yet, and one for what already has. But psychologically, they're deeply connected. Gratitude gives hope its roots. It reminds you of what's carried you so far, which makes it easier to believe in what's coming next.

Why Gratitude Fuels Optimism

When you reflect on what you're thankful for, you're effectively rehearsing resilience. Each memory of something that went right — a challenge overcome, a moment of kindness, a lesson learned — teaches your brain: *I can survive difficulty. Good things still happen.*

This quiet reassurance builds what psychologists call *positive expectancy* — the belief that your efforts can lead to meaningful outcomes. People who practise regular gratitude aren't naïve; they simply have more emotional evidence that life can unfold in their favour.

Optimism, then, isn't about denying difficulty — it's about trusting your capacity to meet it. Gratitude keeps that trust alive.

Anchoring Ambition in Appreciation

Ambition and gratitude might seem like opposites. One reaches forward; the other pauses in the present. But together, they form a balanced rhythm — like breathing in and out.

Without gratitude, ambition becomes restlessness: always striving, never satisfied.
Without ambition, gratitude becomes stagnation: comfortable, but unchallenged.

When you hold both, you create a steady kind of motivation — grounded in appreciation, guided by purpose. You move forward not because you're running from lack, but because you're drawn by vision.

Try asking yourself:

- *What am I already thankful for that points to where I'd like to go next?*

- *What strengths or lessons from my past could help me grow further?*

These questions turn gratitude into direction — a bridge between what's good now and what could be even better.

The Grateful View of Time

Gratitude subtly changes how you perceive time. It softens regret about the past, deepens appreciation for the present, and brings calm to thoughts of the future.

You begin to see that life unfolds in seasons — not everything can bloom at once, and that's okay.

This perspective helps you stop rushing. You start trusting that growth happens gradually and that your future self will thank you for small steps taken today.

That's the quiet power of gratitude: it transforms "What if it doesn't work out?" into "What if it does?"

A Letter to Future You — Planting Seeds of Gratitude and Hope

The future can feel uncertain — and uncertainty often breeds worry. We imagine every possible obstacle, every what-if, and rarely pause to picture what might go *right*.

Gratitude helps to reframe that. It gives you a way to meet the unknown with warmth instead of fear — to see the future not as something to control, but as something to grow into.

One of the most grounding ways to do this is by writing a **letter to your future self.**

Why This Works

When you write to your future self, you're doing two things at once:

1. You're acknowledging your present reality — everything you've already managed, learned, and survived.

2. You're extending belief forward — reminding yourself that growth continues, even when you can't yet see how.

It's an act of *faith in progress*. You're planting gratitude like a seed in the soil of time, trusting it will bloom later.

How to Write Your Letter

You don't need to overthink this — it's not a formal letter, more like a conversation with yourself.

Find a quiet moment, and begin with something like:

"Dear Future Me,

I hope you're proud of how far you've come. Right now, I'm learning to slow down, to notice the good that's already here, and to trust that small steps matter. I don't know exactly what you'll be facing when you read this, but I hope you remember that gratitude has carried you before — and it will carry you again."

You might go on to describe:

- What you're grateful for today

- What values or dreams you want to hold on to

- What you hope your future self remembers when life feels busy or uncertain

The key is to write with kindness, not pressure. You're not demanding perfection from your future self — you're offering reassurance.

The Gratitude Perspective

Writing this letter shifts your attention from anxiety about what might go wrong to gratitude for what might unfold. It reminds you that life isn't something happening *to* you — it's something you're co-creating with each thought and action.

You can even make this a ritual: write a new letter each year and reread the old ones. Notice the growth, the surprises, the unexpected good that found you.

It's a quiet way of proving to yourself that, even when things don't go to plan, you've always found your way through.

A Simple Exercise

Write your letter.
Then seal it — digitally or on paper — and set a reminder to open it in six months or a year.

When that day comes, read it slowly. Notice what came true, what changed, and how much of what you once hoped for has quietly arrived.

That moment of recognition is pure gratitude — not for luck, but for your own endurance, growth, and care.

Trusting the Process — Gratitude as a Guide for What's Ahead

The hardest part of change isn't starting — it's staying the course.
There's a point in every journey where progress feels invisible, and patience starts to run thin. You're showing up, but you can't yet see the result. You're trying, but the reward feels distant.

That's when gratitude becomes your quiet compass.

When you practise gratitude for *process* instead of outcome, you stop measuring life in dramatic milestones and start noticing the value in persistence itself. You learn to trust that growth often happens quietly, beneath the surface, long before you see its shape.

Why the Middle Feels Messy

Every meaningful journey — learning, healing, creating, changing — has a messy middle. It's the part where excitement fades, results are uncertain, and doubt grows loud.

The human brain craves immediate feedback. When we can't see progress, it assumes there isn't any. But growth rarely announces itself; it whispers.

Gratitude helps you listen for those whispers. It turns your attention toward the small signs that things are moving, even slowly:

- The one calm moment in a stressful week.
- The kinder self-talk you didn't notice at first.
- The problem that once derailed you but now only pauses you.

These are the quiet evidences of progress — the roots forming before the blossom. Gratitude teaches you to honour them.

The Calm of Trust

Trust and gratitude share the same heartbeat. Both say: *I don't need all the answers right now.*

When you can be thankful even in uncertainty, you release the need to control every outcome. You start meeting life as a partner, not an opponent.

This doesn't mean becoming passive; it means staying open — acting with hope rather than fear. Gratitude gives you the patience to keep showing up, knowing that every small effort matters, even when the finish line isn't visible yet.

It's the difference between *rushing to arrive* and *allowing yourself to unfold*.

Looking Back With Grace

When you eventually look back on the paths you've walked, you'll realise that the seasons of waiting, confusion, and doubt were just as formative as the moments of success. Gratitude helps you see that.

It reframes struggle as growth, mistakes as learning, and delays as quiet preparation. You begin to trust that every stage had a purpose — that you were always becoming, even when you felt stuck.

Reflection & Action Prompt

Your challenge:
When you feel impatient about progress, pause and name one thing you're grateful for *in this exact stage*.

It might be the lesson, the courage to keep going, or the person walking beside you.

Say to yourself:

"I may not be there yet, but I'm grateful to be becoming."

That single thought turns uncertainty into faith — not blind faith, but faith rooted in evidence: you've made it this far, and gratitude will help you keep going.

Chapter 11 – Gratitude as a Daily Reset

Building a Lifelong Practice

Gratitude is both a feeling and a skill. Feelings come and go — but skills can be strengthened for life.

By now, you've seen how gratitude touches everything: your thoughts, your relationships, your work, your body, even your sense of time. The next step is learning how to *keep it alive.*

A gratitude reset isn't just a one-off experiment; it's a gentle way of living — a daily return to calm, clarity, and appreciation. It's the practice of beginning again, over and over, no matter what life brings.

The Power of Small, Repeated Acts

You don't need grand gestures to maintain gratitude — just small, consistent ones.
Tiny daily acknowledgements build the same neural pathways that shape habits of thought. Over time, they become automatic — your brain begins to look for what's good before it looks for what's wrong.

Think of gratitude as a daily reset button. Each moment of appreciation clears emotional clutter and restores balance.

You might:

- Pause before opening your phone each morning and name one thing you're glad for.

- Keep a small notebook or voice note to capture moments that make you smile.

- Use everyday cues — the kettle boiling, your commute, brushing your teeth — as gentle reminders to notice something good.

It's not about perfection or consistency; it's about *returning*. When you drift away from gratitude (as everyone does), the practice is simply to begin again.

Why Consistency Matters More Than Intensity

People often abandon new habits because they start too big. But gratitude works best in brief, frequent moments. One sentence a day is enough.

Neuroscientists call this *habit stacking* — linking a new action to an existing routine so it becomes natural. For example:

- After you pour your morning coffee, think of one thing you're grateful for.

- Before you close your laptop at the end of work, write one sentence of appreciation for the day.

- As you get into bed, reflect on one small thing that made you feel at peace.

The brain thrives on patterns. Once gratitude becomes part of your existing rhythm, it no longer feels like a task — it becomes part of who you are.

Gratitude as an Emotional Reset

Life will always bring days that feel scattered, pressured, or heavy. Gratitude won't erase them, but it can help you reset more quickly.

When you pause and find even one point of steadiness — a breath, a kind word, a moment of quiet — you interrupt the spiral of stress. Your nervous system shifts from alertness to balance, reminding you: *I'm safe. I'm here. There is still good, even now.*

That's what makes gratitude sustainable. It's not a fair-weather practice; it's a compass you can use in any condition.

Restarting After Setbacks — When Gratitude Slips Away

No matter how strong your intentions, there will be days — or even weeks — when gratitude slips away. You'll get busy, distracted, tired, or overwhelmed. You'll forget to write, or you'll sit with your journal and feel nothing. You might even start wondering if you've lost whatever spark of appreciation you once had.

That's completely normal.

Gratitude isn't a straight line; it's a rhythm — expanding and contracting with the flow of your life. The goal isn't to stay in constant thankfulness, but to *find your way back* when you drift.

Why Setbacks Are Part of Growth

Think of your gratitude practice like a muscle. Each time you forget and then remember, you're strengthening the neural pathways that bring you back faster next time. The forgetting isn't failure — it's training.

In psychology, this is called *reinforcement learning*. The brain learns not just from success, but from repetition — even after breaks. Every return to gratitude reactivates the same circuits of calm, awareness, and emotional balance, making them easier to access in future.

So when you fall out of practice, the most powerful thing you can do is start again — gently, without self-blame.

Let Go of "Perfect" Gratitude

Many people treat gratitude like a checklist — if they don't feel thankful enough, or if their list repeats itself, they believe they're doing it wrong. But gratitude isn't about novelty or constant joy. It's about presence.

If all you can manage is, *"I'm grateful the day is over,"* that's still gratitude.
If you repeat, *"I'm thankful for my bed,"* every night — that's fine too. The point isn't variety; it's awareness.

You don't need to feel grateful to *be* grateful. Some days, noticing is enough.

How to Gently Reset

Here's a simple three-step approach to restarting your gratitude practice:

1. **Pause the judgement.**
   Accept that your practice drifted. Life is full;
   you're human. No guilt required.

2. **Choose one small thing.**
   Find one detail from today that didn't go wrong,
   that gave comfort, or that reminded you you're
   still here.

3. **Name it out loud or write it down.**
   Acknowledge it simply, without forcing feeling:
   "This is something good."

That's it. You've already reset.

The beauty of gratitude is that it doesn't hold grudges.
It's always waiting patiently for you to return.

What Returning Teaches You

Each time you lose your way and begin again, gratitude
deepens.
You start to realise that you don't practise gratitude
because life is perfect — you practise it because it isn't.
You learn that peace isn't the absence of difficulty; it's
the presence of perspective.

Every reset reminds you that you're still growing, still
noticing, still human.
And that awareness, even in the smallest form, *is*
gratitude.

The Ongoing Gift of Gratitude — Living with an Open Heart

Gratitude isn't just something you practise — it
becomes part of how you see the world.

Over time, it shifts from a habit into a way of being: a soft awareness that runs quietly beneath the noise of life.

It's there when things go right, magnifying your joy.
It's there when things go wrong, anchoring you to what still holds.
It's there in the in-between — the pauses, the routines, the moments that pass without applause.

Gratitude becomes your internal light, illuminating even the ordinary.

Gratitude as a Way of Seeing

When gratitude settles into the fabric of your life, you start noticing beauty where you once saw nothing special — the morning light through the window, the familiar sound of footsteps, the comfort of a shared meal.

These aren't dramatic moments. They're the threads that hold your days together. Gratitude simply helps you see them.

It changes how you relate to the world.
Instead of asking, *What's missing?* you begin to ask, *What's already here?*
Instead of waiting for life to be perfect before you feel content, you realise it's already quietly offering you everything you need to feel alive.

That shift — from lack to presence — is where deep peace begins.

A Ripple Effect

Gratitude never ends with you. When you live with an open heart, people feel it.
You listen more fully. You speak more kindly. You appreciate before you criticise.

Your calm becomes contagious — not through words, but through energy.
Each thank you, each moment of noticing, sends out a quiet ripple of steadiness that touches everyone around you.

In this way, gratitude becomes a form of contribution. It shapes the emotional climate of homes, workplaces, and relationships. It turns everyday interactions into opportunities for connection.

The Gift of Returning

There will always be times when gratitude feels distant — when life is too heavy or chaotic to see the good. But gratitude isn't lost in those moments; it's resting.

And when you come back to it, as you always will, it will meet you exactly where you are — without demand, without judgement. That's its gift: unconditional welcome.

Each return deepens your understanding that gratitude isn't about perfection, but about presence. You start to see that being aware — even of your own struggle — is a form of appreciation too.

A Closing Reflection

You've spent these pages learning to notice, appreciate, and return. You've looked back with gentleness, experienced the present with clarity, and begun to see the future with trust.

So take a slow breath.
Notice one thing around you right now that brings ease or warmth.
Hold that awareness for a moment — then whisper a quiet *thank you.*

That's it. That's the whole practice.

Gratitude doesn't need grand words or perfect timing. It only needs you — awake to your own life, willing to see what's already here.

And when you live that way, every day becomes a small reset — a new chance to begin again with an open, grateful heart.

Part Two - Applying Gratitude in Everyday Life

Chapter 12 – Gratitude and Sleep

Rest and Renewal – How Gratitude Calms the Mind Before Sleep

Night-time is meant to be a time of restoration — a natural pause before life begins again.
But for many people, the hours before sleep are anything but peaceful.

You lie down and your body stops moving, but your mind speeds up.
The day replays itself — the things you said, the things you didn't, the worries waiting for tomorrow. The quiet becomes crowded.

It's a familiar pattern: your mind, trained to plan and protect, goes searching for problems to solve. But at night, there's nothing left to *do*. The same alertness that helped you cope during the day now turns against you, keeping rest just out of reach.

Gratitude offers a simple, science-backed way to interrupt that cycle.

Why Gratitude Helps You Sleep

Research from the University of Manchester found that people who keep a nightly gratitude list fall asleep faster, sleep longer, and wake up feeling more refreshed.
It's not magic — it's biology.

When you focus on positive, reassuring thoughts before bed, your brain releases calming neurotransmitters like serotonin and oxytocin. These counteract the stress hormones (like cortisol) that fuel late-night overthinking.

In other words, gratitude tells your nervous system, *you're safe now.*
You move from alertness to ease — from doing to being.

A Gentle Evening Reframe

Instead of lying in bed replaying mistakes or planning tasks, you can use gratitude to shift the story of your day.

Try this:
As you settle down, ask yourself three quiet questions:

1. *What went well today?*

2. *Who or what supported me, even in a small way?*

3. *What did I handle better than I might have before?*

You don't need to write it down unless you want to. Even thinking about your answers softens mental tension and signals to your body that it's safe to rest.

This practice rebalances attention — turning the mind away from problem-solving and toward appreciation. It replaces restlessness with closure.

Sleep as a Form of Gratitude

It's easy to forget that rest itself is an act of gratitude. By allowing your body to recover, you're saying: *thank you for carrying me today; now I'll take care of you in return.*

Sleep isn't wasted time — it's restoration, memory processing, and emotional reset.
When you go to bed with gratitude, you turn sleep into a sacred exchange: effort for renewal, movement for stillness, noise for peace.

Even if you don't fall asleep straight away, the act of thanking the day calms your energy. It's a quiet ritual of completion — a way of saying, *enough for now.*

Bedtime Gratitude Practices – How to Create a Calming Evening Ritual

Evening gratitude doesn't need to be elaborate. In fact, the simpler it is, the more likely it is to become a habit. The goal isn't perfection — it's peace.

Creating a small gratitude ritual at night helps your brain associate bedtime with safety and comfort rather than tension and replay. Over time, this becomes your body's signal to unwind — a transition from *doing* to *being.*

1. The Three Good Things Practice

This is one of the most researched gratitude techniques for improving sleep and wellbeing.

Each night, before bed, think of (or jot down) **three things that went well today**. They don't need to be big:

- A friendly message from someone.
- A meal you enjoyed.

- A quiet moment between tasks.

Then briefly note *why* each one mattered to you. This step deepens the emotional impact — turning gratitude into reflection.

Over time, your brain begins to expect this review, and it starts looking for positive moments throughout the day to "add to the list." You train yourself to notice the good *in real time*, not just at night.

2. Gratitude Breathing

If writing feels too stimulating before bed, try this sensory version instead.

1. Lie comfortably and close your eyes.

2. As you inhale, silently say: *I am thankful for...*

3. As you exhale, finish the thought: *this moment / this breath / this rest.*

You can let the words change naturally — whatever feels true. The rhythm of breathing links with appreciation, calming both body and mind.

This practice anchors gratitude in the body, which helps regulate the nervous system — your breath literally tells your brain, *I'm safe now.*

3. The Gratitude Wind-Down

To help your mind transition from activity to rest, create a small *wind-down ritual* — ten or fifteen minutes before bed. It might include:

- Dimming lights or lighting a candle.

- Writing one sentence in a notebook that starts with, "I'm glad that..."

- Listening to gentle music or nature sounds.

- Reflecting on one person you're thankful for today.

This is your signal to the brain that the day is ending. Just as you brush your teeth or put on pyjamas, gratitude becomes part of your evening hygiene — for the mind instead of the body.

4. Gratitude Body Scan

This final practice blends mindfulness with appreciation.
Lie quietly and bring your attention to one area of your body at a time. As you focus on each part, say a soft thank you — not for how it looks, but for what it does.

"Thank you, feet, for carrying me today."
"Thank you, shoulders, for holding me steady."
"Thank you, eyes, for seeing beauty."

This practice is deeply soothing. It draws awareness away from the day's worries and back into the body, helping you feel grounded, whole, and ready to rest.

Make It Yours

The best evening ritual is one that feels natural. You don't have to do every practice every night — just choose one or two that suit your rhythm.

Some people like to end the day with journalling; others prefer quiet reflection in the dark. What matters is the intention: *to end the day with kindness instead of criticism.*

Gratitude turns bedtime from a restless review into a gentle release — a peaceful way of saying to yourself, *I did enough. I am enough. I can rest now.*

The Science of Calm – How Gratitude Supports Deep Rest and Repair

When you fall asleep feeling calm and safe, your body does more than rest — it repairs.
Sleep is when the brain sorts memories, heals cells, regulates hormones, and clears emotional tension. But this restoration depends on one key condition: the nervous system must first feel *safe enough* to switch off.

That's where gratitude plays its quiet part.

How Gratitude Shifts the Brain

Gratitude activates regions of the brain linked with empathy, pleasure, and emotional regulation — particularly the **prefrontal cortex** and **anterior cingulate cortex**. These areas help quiet the stress responses triggered by the amygdala (the brain's alarm system).

In simple terms: gratitude tells your brain, *you can relax now.*

When you focus on what went right — or even just what didn't go wrong — your body produces more **serotonin** and **dopamine**, both of which help stabilise mood and prepare the body for deep sleep.

Over time, this becomes a feedback loop: the more you end your day with appreciation, the faster your body learns that night-time is a signal for calm.

Gratitude and Heart Rhythms

Research from the HeartMath Institute shows that emotions like appreciation and compassion create a state known as **heart coherence** — where the heart's rhythm becomes smooth and regular.

This coherence improves communication between the heart and brain, triggering relaxation throughout the body.
People who practise gratitude before bed often report feeling physically warmer, calmer, and more settled — because their internal systems are synchronising.

In this way, gratitude doesn't just *feel* good; it literally aligns the body's rhythms for rest and recovery.

Repairing Through Rest

During deep sleep, your brain releases **growth hormone**, which repairs tissue and strengthens the immune system. It also sorts emotional memories, deciding what to keep and what to let go of.

If you go to sleep in a state of stress, your brain stores that tension as priority data — preparing for threat.
If you go to sleep in gratitude, it stores calm instead.
You wake not just rested, but restored.

It's like giving your mind a bedtime instruction: *file the good, release the rest.*

Gratitude as Night-Time Nourishment

Think of gratitude as nutrition for the nervous system. Just as your body needs food to repair itself, your emotions need appreciation to rebalance.

Ending your day with even the smallest note of gratitude is like giving your inner world a warm meal — something to settle, comfort, and sustain you through the night.

It tells your system, *there's enough safety, enough goodness, enough peace to rest now.*

Reflection & Action Prompt

Your challenge:

For one week, choose one small gratitude ritual to practise before bed — journalling, breathing, or a simple thought of thanks.

Each morning, notice how you feel. Are your dreams softer? Do you wake with slightly more clarity or ease?

It's not about perfect sleep — it's about closing each day with a moment of kindness.
Over time, that single act can turn night into a place of renewal, not rumination.

Chapter 13 – Gratitude and Nature

Reconnecting Through the Natural World

In a world of screens, schedules, and speed, nature remains one of the simplest and most reliable sources of calm. Step outside — even for a few minutes — and something shifts. The air feels cooler, the light softer, the mind quieter.

Gratitude and nature belong together because both bring us back to the present. Each encourages awareness, humility, and awe. You don't need a forest or ocean; you just need to *notice* — the movement of clouds, the rhythm of rain, the sound of birds, the scent of soil after rain.

When you connect with the natural world, you're reminded of balance — the way everything in life grows, changes, rests, and renews. Nature doesn't rush, yet it gets everything done.

Gratitude invites you to do the same.

Why Nature Reawakens Appreciation

Spending time in nature — even viewing it through a window — has been shown to reduce stress, lower blood pressure, and improve mood. The Japanese practice of **shinrin-yoku**, or *forest bathing*, is based on this principle: slow, mindful immersion in natural surroundings lowers cortisol and boosts immune function.

But beyond the science, there's something instinctively comforting about being part of the natural world again. You remember that you're not separate from it

— you *are* nature. The same elements that form trees and rivers also live in you: water, breath, rhythm, resilience.

When you look closely at a leaf, a ripple, or a flame, you're witnessing gratitude in motion — the effortless harmony of life sustaining itself.

Small Encounters, Big Shifts

It's easy to underestimate small interactions with nature. You might think you need a long walk in the countryside to feel restored, but even two minutes outdoors can change your physiological state.

Researchers at Cornell University found that just 10 minutes spent in a natural setting — a garden, park, or even a balcony — significantly lowers levels of mental fatigue and improves focus.

That means you can practise nature gratitude anywhere:

- Standing by an open window, breathing in fresh air.

- Watching sunlight shift through trees on your street.

- Listening to rain while you work or rest.

Gratitude magnifies the impact. When you pause to *notice* and *thank* the world around you, your nervous system takes it as evidence that you are safe, connected, and alive.

Nature as a Mirror

The natural world reflects back everything we forget in the rush of daily life.
Trees teach patience. Rivers teach flow. The sky teaches perspective.

Each element has its own quiet wisdom — a reminder that life unfolds in rhythms, not straight lines. Gratitude helps you see these lessons, not as metaphors, but as lived truths.

Nature says: *You don't have to force growth; just create space for it.*
Gratitude replies: *I see what's already blooming.*

Together, they create a dialogue of balance and belonging — a reminder that peace isn't something you build, but something you return to.

Nature as a Teacher of Presence – Learning Stillness and Flow

The natural world is a living classroom in awareness. Everywhere you look, something is quietly demonstrating what it means to *be present*.

A tree doesn't worry about how quickly it's growing.
A river doesn't cling to where it's been or where it's going.
The sky doesn't apologise for its changes.

Each simply *is*. And in that state of being, there's peace — the same peace that gratitude invites you to experience.

What Nature Can Teach Us About Stillness

When you spend time in nature — even for a few minutes — your mind begins to match its rhythm. The nervous system slows. Breathing deepens. Thoughts settle like sediment in clear water.

You begin to notice details that were invisible before: the shape of leaves, the sound of insects, the subtle texture of bark or sand. This slowing of perception is the essence of presence.

It's not forced meditation — it's observation with appreciation.
And when you practise it, you strengthen your capacity to be calm and attentive in everyday life.

Gratitude amplifies this process. When you pair noticing with thankfulness — *thank you for this breeze, this light, this moment* — you transform awareness into connection. You become part of the scene, not separate from it.

Flow: The Natural State of Balance

Just as nature teaches stillness, it also teaches *flow* — the art of moving without resistance.

Everything in the natural world adapts gracefully. A river finds its way around stones; the wind shifts direction without complaint; the tide withdraws only to return.

Gratitude helps you do the same. It reminds you that change isn't loss — it's rhythm. When you trust that rhythm, you stop fighting it. You start meeting life with curiosity instead of control.

You might think of gratitude as your internal current —
guiding you gently forward, no matter what obstacles
appear. Like water, it doesn't need force; it needs faith
in movement.

Letting Nature Recalibrate You

If you're ever unsure where to begin with presence, go
outside and let nature set the pace.

Stand somewhere quiet, if possible, and simply *look*.
Notice the colours, the temperature, the subtle
movements around you. Feel your breath match the
rhythm of what you see — slower, steadier, easier.

In just a few minutes, your internal world starts to align
with the external one. Stress dissolves. Gratitude arises
naturally. You realise that peace isn't something you
have to create — it's something you uncover by slowing
down.

Nature doesn't demand attention; it rewards it.

Simple Outdoor Gratitude Practices – Reconnecting with Calm and Wonder

You don't need hours in the countryside to feel
connected to nature. Even small, mindful moments
outdoors can renew your sense of calm and wonder.

The aim isn't to "do" gratitude perfectly — it's to *notice*.
Each time you pause to see, feel, or hear something
from the natural world, you remind yourself that life
continues, effortlessly, all around you.

These small practices help you remember that peace doesn't require escape; it's available wherever the sky is visible.

1. The Two-Minute Grounding Practice

Step outside — onto grass, pavement, or balcony — and stand still for two minutes.
Feel the ground beneath your feet. Notice its texture, temperature, and steadiness.

As you breathe, silently repeat:

"The earth holds me. I belong here."

This short grounding moment reconnects you to stability. Gratitude naturally follows, because you remember: no matter how much changes, the ground remains.

2. Sky Gratitude

Looking up is one of the simplest ways to reset perspective.
Pause for a moment and notice the sky — its colour, light, clouds, or darkness.

Each glance upward is a reminder of scale: the world is vast, and you are part of something much larger.

You might whisper, *thank you for the reminder that life expands beyond my thoughts*.

Even on grey days, gratitude can be found in the softness of the clouds, the quiet before rain, or the comfort of routine weather patterns.

3. Gratitude Walk

Take a short walk — five minutes if that's all you have. As you move, notice what catches your attention: shapes, scents, sounds, colours. With each step, think or say:

"I'm grateful for this."

The point isn't to analyse — it's to observe and acknowledge. You might notice a bird call, a tree in blossom, or the way light shifts on a wall.

This kind of walk transforms even familiar streets into places of discovery. The world feels more vivid because you're seeing it again, not just passing through it.

4. Seasonal Gratitude

Each season offers its own beauty — freshness, warmth, harvest, stillness.
Try pausing at the start of each new season to name what you're thankful for:

- **Spring:** renewal, light, new beginnings.
- **Summer:** energy, connection, long evenings.
- **Autumn:** colour, reflection, gentle slowing.
- **Winter:** rest, quiet, simplicity.

This practice helps you flow with time instead of resisting it. You begin to see that every phase — in nature and in life — has gifts of its own.

5. Bringing Nature Indoors

If you can't easily spend time outdoors, you can still bring natural calm into your environment:

- Keep a small plant or vase of flowers nearby.

- Play nature sounds while working or resting.

- Open a window and breathe slowly for one minute.

The sensory reminder of life beyond walls is often enough to restore balance and gratitude.

Reflection & Action Prompt

Your challenge:
Spend at least five minutes outdoors today — even if it's just standing by a door or window.
Notice one detail of the natural world that draws your attention, and thank it silently.

"Thank you for reminding me to slow down."

That single pause reconnects you to the rhythm of life — steady, cyclical, endlessly renewing — and to the quiet truth that you are part of something vast, beautiful, and whole.

Chapter 14 – Gratitude and Creativity

Creativity as an Expression of Appreciation

Every act of creativity — from writing a sentence to arranging flowers, painting a wall, or solving a problem — begins with one simple impulse: *to notice.*

You notice a feeling, a pattern, a need, a possibility. You sense something that doesn't yet exist and bring it into being.

That's gratitude in motion.

At its heart, creativity is an act of appreciation — of paying attention to what inspires you, moves you, or deserves to be shared. When you create, you're saying: *This matters. This has meaning.*

Whether it's cooking a meal, designing something new, or capturing a photo, the creative process turns ordinary awareness into expression. Gratitude is what makes that awareness come alive.

Gratitude Opens the Creative Mind

When you feel grateful, your brain shifts into a more open and receptive state. The **dopamine** released during moments of appreciation doesn't just lift mood — it also increases curiosity, imagination, and motivation.

Neuroscientists call this the "broaden-and-build" effect: positive emotions expand your ability to think flexibly and explore ideas. Gratitude, therefore, isn't just a pleasant feeling; it's a creative catalyst.

When you focus on what you appreciate, your attention widens. You see more connections, more beauty, more potential. You stop trying to force inspiration and start allowing it.

This is why so many artists, writers, and thinkers describe their best work as flowing through them, rather than from them. Gratitude creates the mental space for that flow to happen.

Creativity Beyond Art

It's easy to think creativity belongs only to artists, but it lives in everyone.
Creativity is simply the ability to combine things in new ways — a recipe, a conversation, a solution, a plan.

Every time you make a choice that adds beauty, kindness, or efficiency to life, you're creating. And each of those acts can be infused with gratitude.

For example:

- Cooking a meal becomes an act of thanks for nourishment.

- Writing a message becomes gratitude for connection.

- Decorating a space becomes appreciation for comfort.

When you create with awareness, even everyday tasks become expressions of grace. Gratitude gives them meaning.

Creating from Enough, Not from Lack

Many creative blocks come from pressure — the sense that what we make must be perfect, impressive, or productive. Gratitude helps dissolve that tension by reminding you that creativity is already a gift.

You don't have to earn inspiration; you simply have to notice it.
When you create from appreciation instead of expectation, you move from striving to enjoyment.

This is the creative paradox: when you stop forcing greatness, genuine inspiration begins.

Gratitude says, *I'm already enough, and what I make doesn't need to prove it.*
From that space, ideas unfold naturally — because they're expressions of joy, not judgement.

Overcoming Blocks Through Gratitude – Finding Courage to Create Again

Every creative person — and that includes everyone — eventually meets resistance.
You sit down to start something and suddenly doubt appears:
What if it's not good enough? What if I'm not good enough?

The inner critic wakes up, and before you've begun, you've stopped.

Gratitude can be a surprisingly powerful antidote to that fear. Not because it silences the voice of doubt completely, but because it changes your relationship with it. It softens self-judgement into self-compassion, allowing creativity to breathe again.

Why Fear Blocks Flow

Creativity and fear share the same stage. They both live in the imagination — one envisions possibilities, the other predicts problems.

When fear takes over, the brain's **amygdala** activates, flooding your body with stress hormones that narrow focus and limit curiosity. You enter survival mode, and creativity shuts down.

Gratitude reverses this pattern. When you focus on what's working — what you've learned, what you've enjoyed, what you're capable of — your nervous system relaxes. Dopamine and serotonin rise, making exploration feel safe again.

It's not about pretending everything's fine; it's about remembering that progress has already happened, and it will happen again.

Gratitude gives you evidence of resilience.

Reframing the Inner Critic

Next time that critical voice whispers, "Who do you think you are?" try answering with gratitude:

"I'm someone who's trying. I'm thankful I have the chance to learn."

That one sentence changes the emotional tone immediately.
You move from defence to openness — from perfectionism to permission.

Gratitude doesn't argue with the critic; it outgrows it. It reminds you that creative effort itself is something to

celebrate. You don't have to earn the right to create —
you already have it.

Finding Gratitude in the Process

Perfectionism focuses on the result. Gratitude focuses
on the experience.

When you let go of how things *should* look and start
appreciating what it feels like to *make* something, you
rediscover joy.

Try this:
When creating — writing, painting, gardening, solving
a problem — pause occasionally and ask,

"What part of this process am I grateful for right now?"

It could be the colours, the quiet, the satisfaction of
solving a small problem. Each moment of appreciation
keeps your focus anchored in flow rather than
outcome.

Courage Through Appreciation

Courage doesn't mean you stop being afraid; it means
you create anyway.
Gratitude gives you the strength to do that because it
shifts your attention from fear of failure to love of
expression.

When you're grateful simply to have the opportunity to
create — to play, explore, and share — the need to be
perfect fades. What remains is joy, movement, and
growth.

Creativity doesn't thrive on pressure. It thrives on
appreciation.

Every brushstroke, word, or idea becomes a quiet declaration: *I'm thankful to be here, making something new.*

Finding Flow and Joy in Making – Gratitude as Creative Fuel

When creativity feels good, time disappears. The world narrows to the brushstroke, the paragraph, the melody, the movement of hands. You're no longer worrying about how it will turn out — you're simply immersed in the making.

That's the state psychologists call **flow** — total absorption in what you're doing. It's deeply satisfying, calming, and energising all at once. And gratitude is one of the easiest gateways to enter it.

When you're thankful for the opportunity to create, your focus naturally shifts from pressure to presence. You stop chasing results and start savouring the process. Every movement becomes a meditation.

Gratitude Invites Flow

Flow happens when three things align: focus, enjoyment, and freedom from self-judgement. Gratitude supports all three.

1. **Focus** – Gratitude anchors you in the moment, pulling attention away from distractions.

2. **Enjoyment** – Appreciation increases dopamine, which fuels intrinsic motivation — the pleasure of doing something for its own sake.

3. **Freedom** – Gratitude loosens the grip of perfectionism; you stop needing approval and start experiencing wonder.

In that state, creativity isn't effort — it's expression.

Returning to Play

Gratitude has a childlike quality: curious, delighted, unguarded. When you bring that spirit into your creative life, even serious projects regain their sense of play.

Think of a child drawing — they don't worry about whether it's "good." They enjoy the colours, the shapes, the act of creating something that didn't exist before.

Gratitude lets adults rediscover that freedom. When you stop measuring, comparing, or rushing, you find joy again in small details — the smell of paint, the rhythm of typing, the simple satisfaction of making.

Play doesn't mean immaturity; it means presence without pressure.

Refuelling Creative Energy

It's natural for creative energy to ebb and flow. When inspiration feels low, gratitude can refuel it.

Try this:
Look back at something you've made before — a project, a meal, a letter, a plan — and instead of criticising it, thank it.

"Thank you for teaching me."
"Thank you for showing me what I can do."

That shift changes memory into motivation. You remind yourself that creativity isn't a one-time spark; it's a renewable source.

The more you appreciate your own process, the more inspiration begins to reappear — not because you forced it, but because you *welcomed* it.

The Joy of Simply Making

In the end, creativity is an act of connection — to yourself, to others, to the world. Each time you make something with gratitude, you leave a small trace of beauty behind.

It doesn't have to be perfect to be worthwhile. What matters is that it exists — that you gave shape to something that moved you.

Gratitude turns every act of creation into celebration: of your senses, your effort, your imagination. It transforms making into meaning.

Reflection & Action Prompt

Your challenge:
This week, create something — anything — just for the joy of it.
Don't aim for usefulness or applause. Write a note, arrange flowers, doodle, cook, hum, move.

Then pause, notice how it feels, and say to yourself:

"I'm grateful I can create."

That single thought is the essence of creative flow — gratitude turned into movement, presence turned into art.

Part Three – Living the Reset

Chapter 15 – The 30-Day Gratitude Reset Plan

Why 30 Days?

Change doesn't happen overnight. Research shows that new habits typically take **between 21–66 days** to become automatic. Thirty days is long enough to experience real shifts, but short enough to feel achievable.

Think of this plan as a reset button for your life. Over the next month, you'll gradually re-train your brain to notice, savour, and express gratitude—not as an occasional task, but as a way of living.

How to Use This Plan

- **Set aside 5–10 minutes daily.** That's all you need.

- **Keep a journal or notes app.** Writing anchors the practice more deeply.

- **Go gently.** Miss a day? That's okay. Just pick up where you left off.

- **Reflect weekly.** Each week has a theme—take a few minutes to notice how the practices are shaping you.

Week 1: Awakening Awareness (Days 1–7)

The first week is about noticing. You'll learn to pause, pay attention, and spot gratitude in small places.

- **Day 1:** Write down 3 things you're grateful for right now.

- **Day 2:** Gratitude using your senses: one sight, one sound, one smell.

- **Day 3:** Name one thing you're grateful for in your body.

- **Day 4:** Notice one small joy during a routine task.

- **Day 5:** Take a gratitude walk—find 3 things outside to appreciate.

- **Day 6:** Thank yourself for one thing you managed this week.

- **Day 7:** Reflection: How did noticing change your week?

Week 2: Expanding Outward (Days 8–14)

This week focuses on relationships and connection. Gratitude strengthens bonds and creates ripple effects.

- **Day 8:** Write down 3 people who have supported you.

- **Day 9:** Send a thank-you message to one person.

- **Day 10:** Share gratitude aloud at dinner or with a friend.

- **Day 11:** Write about one person who inspires you (past or present).

- **Day 12:** Thank someone for an "ordinary" thing they do.

- **Day 13:** Practise gratitude in conflict—what do you still value about the person?

- **Day 14:** Reflection: How did expressing gratitude affect your connections?

Week 3: Deepening the Practice (Days 15–21)

Here, gratitude moves from surface-level to deeper layers: challenges, resilience, and meaning.

- **Day 15:** Write 3 gratitudes from today—even if the day was tough.

- **Day 16:** Reframe one difficulty: what did it teach you, or what support did you receive?

- **Day 17:** Gratitude for past resilience—list 3 challenges you overcame.

- **Day 18:** Thank your body for one way it carried you today.

- **Day 19:** Write down one mistake you made and what you're grateful it taught you.

- **Day 20:** Gratitude in stillness—spend 5 minutes breathing, whispering "thank you."

- **Day 21:** Reflection: How has gratitude changed the way you view hard moments?

Week 4: Living the Reset (Days 22–30)

This final week is about embedding gratitude into everyday life so it becomes a lasting habit.

- **Day 22:** Anchor gratitude to a daily routine (coffee, brushing teeth, bedtime).

- **Day 23:** Practise gratitude at work—thank a colleague or notice one positive.

- **Day 24:** Gratitude for nature—find 3 details outside to appreciate.

- **Day 25:** Gratitude for creativity—thank yourself for one idea or expression.

- **Day 26:** Try a bedtime gratitude ritual to ease into sleep.

- **Day 27:** Write a gratitude letter to your future self.

- **Day 28:** Share one week's worth of gratitudes with someone you trust.

- **Day 29:** Collect your top 10 gratitudes from the whole month.

- **Day 30:** Reflection: Write how you've changed—and one way you'll keep gratitude alive.

Tips for Success

- **Keep it real.** Don't force "big" gratitudes. Small and ordinary is enough.

- **Be specific.** Instead of "I'm grateful for family," try "I'm grateful for my sister's laugh on the phone today."

- **Feel it.** Don't just write—pause to notice the warmth or calm the gratitude brings.

- **Make it yours.** Adapt prompts if needed. The point is connection, not perfection.

What to Expect After 30 Days

If you commit to this reset, you'll likely notice:

- A calmer, more balanced mind

- More patience in daily life

- Stronger bonds in relationships

- Better sleep and lower stress

- A natural ability to spot joy in ordinary places

Most importantly, you'll have built the foundations of a lifelong gratitude practice—one that carries you far beyond these 30 days.

Final Encouragement

Remember: this isn't about getting it right. It's about showing up, one day at a time, with a willingness to notice, to thank, and to live a little more awake to the good that surrounds you.

Gratitude isn't a destination. It's a reset you can return to, over and over, no matter what life brings.

Chapter 16 – Living with Gratitude

Living the Reset – Gratitude as a Way of Life

At first, gratitude feels like something you *do*.
You write in a journal, pause before meals, whisper a quiet "thank you" before sleep. It's deliberate — a choice, a practice, an experiment.

But over time, something subtle changes. The habit becomes a rhythm, and the rhythm becomes a way of seeing. Gratitude shifts from effort to instinct. You start to notice beauty without searching for it. You find yourself saying thank you without prompting.

This is what it means to *live the reset*.

Beyond the Practice

You don't need a list, a notebook, or even a perfect morning routine to live with gratitude. Those tools are helpful — they train your awareness — but the goal is freedom, not discipline.

When gratitude takes root, it follows you naturally:

- Into the kitchen, when you notice the simple pleasure of making tea.

- Into your relationships, when you pause before reacting and choose kindness instead.

- Into quiet moments, when you realise that being alive, right now, is enough.

Gratitude becomes less about doing and more about *being*. It's woven into the way you look, listen, and respond.

The Gentle Power of Perspective

Living with gratitude doesn't mean pretending everything is easy. Life will always bring challenge and change. But gratitude softens your focus — it keeps you aware of light even when shadows appear.

When you practise appreciation through difficulty, you're not denying pain; you're expanding context. You're reminding yourself that even in hard moments, something steady remains — the breath, the sky, the love that persists despite circumstance.

Gratitude doesn't erase suffering. It balances it. It helps you see that life is wide enough to hold both — joy and sorrow, success and struggle, endings and beginnings.

That awareness becomes a quiet strength — a calm confidence that whatever happens, you can return to the simple truth of *enough*.

Living the Reset Every Day

To live with gratitude is to remember that each day can begin again — not perfectly, but honestly.
You won't always wake feeling thankful. Some mornings, gratitude will feel distant. But every day offers another chance to notice, to pause, to start again.

That's what the word *reset* really means — not to erase, but to realign.
Each time you return to gratitude, you realign your perspective with peace.

Living the reset is about choosing awareness over autopilot, compassion over criticism, and appreciation over accumulation. It's not grand; it's grounded.

153

And the beauty of it is this: the more you live with gratitude, the lighter everything else becomes.

Gratitude in Motion – Carrying It Forward into Life, Work, and Relationships

When gratitude becomes part of who you are, it naturally begins to move outward.
It colours how you speak, how you listen, how you respond.
It turns daily interactions into quiet exchanges of warmth and respect — not because you're trying to be positive, but because appreciation has become your resting state.

Gratitude at Work

In professional life, gratitude often gets mistaken for weakness — as if appreciation means you're too soft, too sentimental. In reality, it's one of the strongest forces for productivity and trust.

When you thank a colleague, you're not just being polite; you're acknowledging effort. Recognition creates motivation — a sense that what we do matters. Gratitude transforms workplaces because it builds belonging.

Even when your job feels demanding, a simple practice can shift your focus:
At the end of each workday, ask yourself,

"What part of today added value — to me, to others, or to something bigger?"

That single reflection helps you end the day with meaning rather than fatigue.

Gratitude in Relationships

In relationships, gratitude works like sunlight — small, consistent warmth that keeps connection alive.

It's easy to take people for granted when life gets busy. But appreciation is what nourishes trust. You don't need grand gestures; you just need attention.

Notice when someone helps you, listens, or makes life easier. Say something simple:

"I noticed what you did — thank you."

Moments like that create safety. Gratitude softens defensiveness, making it easier to communicate and forgive. It turns daily routines — making tea, folding laundry, sharing a meal — into small rituals of care.

Over time, this becomes the emotional heartbeat of your relationships: steady, kind, alive.

Gratitude in Life's Rhythm

Living with gratitude doesn't mean constant excitement. Some days will feel flat or heavy, and that's part of the rhythm too. Gratitude in motion adapts — it flows through your current reality rather than fighting it.

On bright days, gratitude feels like joy.
On quiet days, it feels like peace.
On hard days, it feels like endurance — the ability to say, *even now, something good remains.*

When gratitude becomes a rhythm rather than a ritual, you start to move through life with more ease. You handle change with curiosity instead of panic. You forgive faster. You laugh more.

That's gratitude in motion: not a feeling you chase, but a perspective you carry.

A Life of Appreciation – The Lasting Gift of Gratitude

When you look back over this journey, you'll notice that gratitude hasn't changed the *facts* of your life — it's changed how you see them.
The same world looks softer now. The same routines feel gentler. The same challenges seem more manageable, because you've learned how to meet them with awareness instead of reaction.

Gratitude hasn't erased difficulty, but it has widened your view.
It's given you the ability to hold both — the ache and the beauty, the chaos and the calm.

And that balance is what makes life richer.

The Subtle Transformation

The biggest transformations are often the quietest. You may not notice them at first — the way you breathe more deeply, smile more easily, recover more quickly from stress.

But over time, you'll realise: something within you has softened.
You move through your days with more grace. You pause a little more often. You find joy in moments that used to pass unnoticed.

That's what living with gratitude feels like — not constant happiness, but a steady hum of contentment. A sense that, even when life isn't perfect, it's still precious.

The Ongoing Reset

The "reset" in this book was never about starting over completely. It was about remembering — again and again — that peace and clarity are always within reach.

Each time you feel overwhelmed, return to what you've learned:
Pause. Notice. Appreciate.

You can begin again at any moment — during a walk, a meal, a breath.
That's the gift of gratitude: it never expires, never demands, never leaves. It's always waiting quietly for your attention.

Every new day is an invitation to practise — not out of obligation, but out of love.

The Quiet Legacy of Gratitude

When you live this way, your gratitude touches others without effort.
Your calm becomes reassuring. Your kindness becomes contagious.
You become, simply by being yourself, a source of light in your corner of the world.

That is the true legacy of gratitude — not what you achieve, but how you make others feel in your presence.

And perhaps, without even realising it, that's how you change the world: one moment of appreciation at a time.

A Final Reflection

Take a deep breath. Look around.
There is something, right now, to be thankful for.

It might be the air in your lungs, the quiet in the room,
or the fact that you're here — reading these words,
ready to live more fully.

Let that awareness settle. Let it fill you.

You don't need to chase gratitude anymore.
You're already living it.

A Note from the Author

If you've made it to this final page, thank you — truly.

Writing this book has been a reminder that gratitude isn't something we master once and for all; it's something we keep returning to, like a trusted friend. There were days I felt calm and thankful, and days when appreciation felt far away — but each time I paused, breathed, and noticed something small, I found my way back again.

That's the heart of *The Gratitude Reset*: not perfection, but presence.

My hope is that these pages have helped you rediscover that feeling too — the quiet peace that comes when you stop chasing "more" and start seeing what's already here.
Whether you began this journey to lift your mood, reconnect with yourself, or simply to feel a little lighter, I hope you've realised that gratitude was never something to *add* to your life — it's something that was already within you, waiting to be noticed.

So please, keep practising in your own way.
Write when you can. Pause when you remember.
Be gentle with yourself when you forget.

Gratitude will always be there when you return.

And if this book has helped you — even a little — to breathe more deeply, to slow down, or to find joy in the small and ordinary, then it's done its job.

Thank you for sharing this journey with me.
May your days be full of simple moments worth noticing —
and the awareness to see them as the gifts they are.

With warmth and appreciation,
Amelia Walsh

Acknowledgements

This book, like all in the *Everyday Reset* series, was shaped by small moments of encouragement, support, and inspiration — from both the people closest to me and the readers who continue to remind me why gratitude matters.

To everyone who has shared their own stories of change, calm, and clarity — thank you. Your words, messages, and quiet reflections have become part of these pages in ways you may never realise.

To my family and friends — thank you for your patience, humour, and grounding presence through the writing process. For every cup of tea, every walk, every moment of gentle perspective — I'm endlessly grateful.

And to you, the reader — thank you for choosing to spend your time here. Your willingness to pause, reflect, and practise awareness is what gives this work meaning.

May these words meet you exactly where you need them,
and may gratitude continue to guide your days —
softly, steadily, and with light.

With love and appreciation,
Amelia Walsh

About the Author

Amelia Walsh is the author of *The Everyday Reset* series — a collection of simple, uplifting guides designed to help readers create calm, clarity, and confidence through small daily changes.

Her work blends gentle psychology with practical lifestyle habits, encouraging a return to balance in an often over-busy world.
Each book offers a reminder that transformation doesn't begin with grand gestures, but with small, steady moments of awareness.

Amelia's approachable style and grounded optimism have helped thousands of readers rediscover peace, gratitude, and joy in everyday life.

When she's not writing, she can usually be found walking by the coast, journalling in cafés, or spending quiet time outdoors — practising the very resets she writes about.

Also by Amelia Walsh

The Everyday Reset Series

- **The Gratitude Reset**
  A 30-Day Mood-Boosting Practice

- **The Decluttering Reset**
  Simple Steps to Clear Space, Reduce Stress, and Simplify Your Life for Good

- **The Walking Reset**
  Simple Steps to Boost Mood, Improve Health, and Build a Daily Habit That Lasts

- **The Connection Reset**
  Rebuilding Meaningful Relationships with Friends, Family, and Community

- **The Sleep Reset**
  Restorative Rituals to Calm the Mind and Improve Rest Naturally

- **The Energy Reset**
  Practical Ways to Recharge, Refocus, and Feel Vibrant Every Day

- **The Everyday Reset**
  Small Changes, Big Shifts – Your Guide to a Calmer, Happier Life

A Final Request

Thank you so much for spending this time with *The Gratitude Reset*. I hope the practices and reflections have brought you moments of calm, connection, and joy.

If you found this book helpful, the best way you can support it is by leaving a short review on Amazon. Reviews make a huge difference—they help other readers discover the book and decide whether it's the right fit for them.

Your words don't need to be long or detailed. Just a few honest sentences about what you enjoyed or how the book helped you will mean so much.

With gratitude,

Amelia

Printed in Dunstable, United Kingdom

70029106R00100